Myths and Realities of Foreign Investment in Poor Countries

THE MODERN LEVIATHAN IN THE THIRD WORLD

John M. Rothgeb, Jr.

PRAEGER

New York
Westport, Connecticut
London

Library of Congress Cataloging-in-Publication Data

Rothgeb, John M.
    Myths and realities of foreign investment in poor countries : the
modern leviathan in the Third World / John M. Rothgeb, Jr.
        p. cm.
    Bibliography: p.
    Includes index.
    ISBN 0–275–93255–9 (alk. paper)
    1. Investments, Foreign—Developing countries.   2. International
business enterprises—Developing countries.   I. Title.
    HG5993.R67   1989
    332.6'73'091724—dc19   88–34026

Library of Congress Catalog Card Number: 88–34026
ISBN: 0–275–93255–9

First published in 1989

Praeger Publishers, One Madison Avenue, New York, NY 10010
A division of Greenwood Press, Inc.

Printed in the United States of America

The paper used in this book complies with the Permanent
Paper Standard issued by the National Information Standards
Organization (Z39.48—1984).

10 9 8 7 6 5 4 3 2 1

Copyright Acknowledgment

    Chapter 2 is based upon work by this author that was previously reported in "Trojan Horse,
Scapegoat, or Non–Foreign Entity: Foreign Policy and Investment Penetration in Poor Countries,"
Journal of Conflict Resolution 31 (June 1987): 227–65.

Myths and Realities
of Foreign Investment
in Poor Countries

Contents

Tables

Acknowledgments

Many people have played an important role both in helping me to prepare this book and during the course of my career. Maurice A. East has been a close friend and a superb mentor. I quite literally would have accomplished nothing without Mickey's help and guidance. Frank C. Zagare and Jacek Kugler have been good friends and colleagues. They encouraged me to undertake this project, and they gave me assistance when I needed it most. Steven M. DeLue has been an understanding department chairman. One could not ask to work with a finer person. In addition, my family has been a source of immeasurable support. My wife, Sue, listened carefully while I outlined many of the arguments found in this book and helped me to explore their shortcomings. She also did the bulk of the typing and editing. Her help was absolutely essential. My son, Johnny, was patient and quiet when necessary and cheerfully tolerated many long hours when his parents were engaged in work. My mother, Carrie Lee, displayed a keen interest in my work that helped inspire me to continue through to the conclusion.

I wish to express my sincere appreciation to each of these people and to the many others who helped me along the way.

Myths and Realities of Foreign Investment in Poor Countries

1

Introduction

One of the often-found themes in the international relations literature is that many new actors have emerged recently and now play an important role in world politics.[1] Among these new actors is the multinational corporation. Vernon (1971:4–11) defines the multinational corporation as a cluster of businesses joined together by bonds of common ownership and able to exploit a common pool of resources. Such corporations have a headquarters in one country, known as the home state, and subsidiaries in other countries, known as host states. The investments made abroad by these firms primarily are direct, in that the corporation retains significant managerial control over the facilities and resources acquired as a result of the flow of capital.[2]

The direct investments across international borders that are made by multinational firms are increasingly seen as important links binding states to one another and as having possibly vast political, social, and economic implications both for the society receiving the investments and for the state from which the investments originate. Indeed, the consequences of multinational corporate behavior appear to be so immensely important that one is tempted to label such firms as modern leviathans that may rival the traditional leviathans, or states, that have for scores of decades dominated the international scene.

Whether these corporations are in fact credible challengers to the state is a matter of considerable controversy. For the most part, analysts see these firms as far from omnipotent when they deal with advanced industrial core states (for example, see Vernon, 1981:517), noting that the firm depends upon such states for an international atmosphere that is orderly and conducive to transactions across international borders (Gilpin, 1975; Krasner, 1976). Many scholars argue, however, that the consequences of corporate behavior are far different when one considers the impact of multinational firms upon underdeveloped societies, main-

Table 1.1

Total Sales and Net Income of the World's Twenty Largest Corporations in 1975 (in millions of U.S. dollars)

Corporation	Total Sales	Net Income
Exxon	44,864	2,503
General Motors	35,725	1,253
Royal Dutch/Shell Group	32,105	2,110
Texaco	24,507	830
Ford Motor Company	24,009	323
Mobil Oil	20,620	810
National Iranian Oil	18,854	16,947
British Petroleum	17,286	369
Standard Oil of California	16,822	772
Unilever	15,016	322
International Business Machines	14,436	1,990
Gulf Oil	14,268	700
General Electric	13,399	580
Chrysler	11,699	-259
International Telephone and Telegraph	11,368	398
Philips Gloeilampenfabrieken	10,746	152
Standard Oil (Indiana)	9,955	787
Cie Francaise des Petroles	9,146	168
Nippon Steel	8,797	112
August Thyssen - Hutte	8,765	100

Source: *Fortune*, August 1976.

taining that the strength of the corporation is such that it is very difficult for these states to compete effectively and to control the activities of firms operating within their borders (see Biersteker, 1980; Weinstein, 1976).

Rothgeb (1986a:126–27) attributes much of the impact of multinational corporations on Third World states to the resources that they have available. In particular, such firms are seen as possessing vast pools of capital, technology, and entrepreneurial talent of the sort that are essential to the development of underdeveloped societies (see Barnet and Muller, 1974:133–47; Vernon, 1977:139–75). The immensity of the resources of these corporations is illustrated in Tables 1.1 to 1.4, which compare the total sales and profits of the 20 largest multinational firms in 1975 and 1980 with the gross domestic product (GDP) of 20 of the largest and 20 of the smallest Third World states for the same years.[3] In 1975, the total sales of the largest corporation, Exxon, constituted 36.1% of the total GDP of the largest of the states in the Third World, Brazil, and was 153 times the size of the total GDP of the smallest of these states, South Yemen. The combined total sales of the 20 largest corporations was 44.4% of the combined total GDP of the largest 20 countries and was 30.1 times the size of the combined total GDP of the smallest 20 countries. In 1980, Exxon's total sales constituted 41.3% of Brazil's total GDP and was 154 times the size of South Yemen's total GDP. The combined total sales of the largest 20 corporations was 46% of the combined total GDP of the largest 20 countries and was 22.1 times the size of the combined total GDP of the smallest 20 countries.

Table 1.2
Total Gross Domestic Product of Selected Underdeveloped Countries in 1975
(in millions of U.S. dollars)

Top Twenty		Bottom Twenty	
Brazil	124,277	South Yemen	292
Spain	104,836	Laos	300
India	88,448	Central African Republic	397
Mexico	88,004	Burundi	415
Yugoslavia	54,585	Mauritania	477
Iran	51,924	Somalia	492
Argentina	39,672	Mongolia	519
Turkey	35,949	Benin	528
Nigeria	34,483	Rwanda	568
Indonesia	30,464	Mali	574
Venezuela	27,561	Cambodia	592
South Korea	20,561	Togo	599
Philippines	15,812	Malawi	613
Peru	15,377	Burkina Faso	674
Portugal	14,724	Haiti	681
Thailand	14,663	Sierra Leone	682
Algeria	14,362	Chad	693
Iraq	13,635	Niger	842
Egypt	13,419	Jordan	1,007
Pakistan	13,338	North Yemen	1,082

Source: U.N., Yearbook of National Accounts Statistics, vol. 2.

Table 1.3
Total Sales and Net Income of the World's Twenty Largest Corporations in 1980
(in millions of U.S. dollars)

Corporation	Total Sales	Net Income
Exxon	103,143	5,650
Royal Dutch / Shell Group	77,114	5,174
Mobil	59,510	3,272
General Motors	57,728	-762
Texaco	51,196	2,642
British Petroleum	48,036	3,337
Standard Oil of California	40,479	2,401
Ford Motor Company	37,085	-1,543
E.N.I.	27,187	98
Gulf Oil	26,483	1,407
International Business Machines	26,213	3,562
Standard Oil (Indiana)	26,133	1,915
Fiat	25,155	NA
General Electric	24,959	1,514
Francaise des Petroles	23,940	946
Atlantic Richfield	23,744	1,651
Unilever	23,607	658
Shell Oil	19,830	1,542
Renault	18,979	160
Petroleos de Venezuela	18,819	3,450

NA = not available.
Source: *Fortune*, August 1981.

Table 1.4
Total Gross Domestic Product of Selected Underdeveloped Countries in 1980
(in millions of U.S. dollars)

Top Twenty		Bottom Twenty	
Brazil	249,725	South Yemen	668
Spain	211,781	Mauritania	691
India	162,138	Central African Republic	796
Argentina	153,331	Burundi	889
Mexico	134,511	Benin	1,035
Iran	86,645	Togo	1,130
Nigeria	85,111	Rwanda	1,163
Indonesia	72,482	Sierra Leone	1,231
South Korea	58,246	Malawi	1,245
Turkey	56,918	Burkina Faso	1,333
Yugoslavia	55,333	Mali	1,422
Venezuela	48,390	Haiti	1,454
Algeria	42,105	Nicaragua	2,178
Greece	40,147	Honduras	2,488
Philippines	35,426	Niger	2,513
Iraq	34,158	Papua New Guinea	2,533
Thailand	33,450	Jamaica	2,660
Colombia	33,400	North Yemen	2,768
Pakistan	28,485	Senegal	2,970
Chile	27,571	Madagascar	3,192

Source: U.N., Yearbook of National Accounts Statistics, vol. 2.

As these figures indicate, multinational corporations clearly have a powerful financial foundation from which to conduct their operations. Of course, not all corporate resources are liquid and readily usable, and those that are available are spread over a variety of states, both developed and developing. Hence, any particular Third World state must deal with only a portion of the total pool of corporate resources, and the disparity in strength may not be as great as one might suppose at first. At the same time, however, one should realize that Third World governments have access to only a portion of their total GDP. Thus, while corporations may not be as powerful as the figures indicate, neither are the host governments. Moreover, firms usually operate from corporate bases in the advanced industrialized states and have access to educational institutions, research and development facilities, pools of managerial talent, and so forth, that often are not available to underdeveloped states. Indeed, poor countries may turn to multinational corporations as sources for these resources, providing such firms with even greater potential leverage.

Given these considerations, the hot, and often raging, debate among scholars that surrounds the role of the multinational corporation in Third World states may be only natural. Depending upon the author one consults, these firms are attributed with the power to solve many of the problems confronting host governments and to contribute significantly to development, or to exacerbate those difficulties and postpone development indefinitely. On the one hand, Barnet and Muller (1974:148–84) note the often-heard claim that foreign firms may serve as "engines of development," helping poor societies catch up with developed states. Diaz-Alejandro (1970:322) maintains that "most of these [foreign] investments had, on balance, a positive economic impact on host countries," and Ranis (1976:99) argues that "foreign capital and management can provide an important assist" to underdeveloped states. Reuber (1973:37, 151–52) agrees with these conclusions, regarding foreign firms as a source of capital and of technological and managerial competence and as spurring the growth of local businesses that complement the activities of the foreigners.

On the other hand, the investments made by foreign firms are seen by many as having pernicious effects upon host states that are poor. Bodenheimer (1971:162–63) discusses many of these negative effects:

1. Foreign investors seize control over the most dynamic and strategically important sectors of the host economy.

2. Foreign enterprises undermine and destroy the locally owned firms found in the host society.

3. Foreigners rob host states of the capital needed for development by repatriating profits to their home states.

4. Foreigners distort host economies by forcing them to fit into the international profit-making schemes followed by multinational firms.

5. Foreign firms introduce capital-intensive technology that is ill-suited to the needs of an underdeveloped society.

6. Foreigners restrict closely the transfer of technology to the host society, thereby depriving it of an ability to begin self-sustained development.

7. Multinational firms hurt the trading positions of host states by creating a demand for high-cost foreign technology.

Galeano (1971:210–16) adds that higher levels of foreign investment in a poor society result in lower rates of economic growth and provide foreigners with undue influence over host state public policy, which may be molded to suit the best interests of foreigners instead of the needs of the local population. Barnet and Muller (1974:163–65) also point to several detrimental effects, including a brain drain that occurs as foreign firms siphon off local talent by employing it and transferring it abroad, the sale to host states of obsolete technology at exorbitant prices, the destruction of local jobs, and the encouragement of a consumer-oriented development strategy that is not in the best long-term interests of the host country. Reuber (1973:20–21), Moore (1973:25–26), and Vernon (1977:144–45) note that charges of this sort are frequently made by those who are critical of multinational corporations.

The dispute regarding the relationship between multinational corporations and underdeveloped countries goes far deeper, however, and reflects fundamental differences of opinion regarding the very structure of the international system and the basic relationships between advanced and poor countries. Chase-Dunn (1975:720–26), Portes (1976:61–82), McGowan and Smith (1978:183–85), and

Jackman (1982:176–82) point to the existence of several schools of thought. Foreign investments are seen variously as a part of an international structure for controlling the weak, as a mechanism for transferring capitalism from developed to underdeveloped states, and as a consequence of the operation of a decentralized international arena. For example, Magdoff (1969:12–15) sees multinational corporations as the most important tool of contemporary imperialism and regards foreign investments in underdeveloped societies as a part of an overall scheme whereby modern capitalist states dominate and control host countries, guaranteeing themselves access to cheap raw materials and important markets. O'Connor (1970:141) echoes this theme, stating that "the multinational corporation has become the instrument for the creation and consolidation of an international ruling class."

Barnet and Muller (1974:55–60) disagree. Although they are critical of multinational corporations, these authors believe that such firms clearly are not agents of imperialism, contending that while they may have a deleterious impact on host underdeveloped countries, these effects are a product of the firm's quest for profits and the absence of any international structures designed to regulate its behavior. Indeed, it is argued that multinational enterprises seek to avoid too close an association or identification with any particular state:

To function successfully on a global scale, a company must not appear to be an extension of any nation-state. It is now commonplace . . . that management not put the welfare of any country in which it does business above that of any other. (Barnet and Muller, 1974:56–57).

Moore (1973:25) and Vernon (1976:47–48) agree that the search for profits, and not the maintenance of an international structure of imperialism, is the basic motivation behind corporate behavior in Third World states.

For those interested in understanding the manner in which international forces affect underdeveloped countries and who wish to promote policies that will increase the probability of development in poor societies, these basic disagreements are both discouraging and confusing. One is left to wonder whether the promotion of foreign investment is a reasonable option that will lead to growth and development, or whether it merely will compound the myriad problems already confronted by the underdeveloped and enmesh them in an international web of domination. Confronted with economics and societies that are plagued by severe difficulties, many Third World leaders often see foreign investment as a panacea and turn to multinational corporations for the investments that they hope will lead to growth and prosperity. If the critics of foreign investment are correct, then this is a fundamental mistake based on an illusion. Instead of seeking such investment as a solution, such states should attempt to eliminate it, for it causes or compounds many of their problems. If the critics are wrong, then promoting foreign investment may be a good policy choice.

From a more theoretical point of view, understanding the role played by foreign investment is of importance for determining how international forces affect the members of the international system and the degree to which a state's foreign and domestic policy behavior and the social processes found within a society are affected by factors originating in the state's external environment. The examination of foreign investments in underdeveloped countries is especially well suited for these purposes, for Rothgeb (1986b:130) notes that foreign investments are among the strongest of the international factors that may affect a state, and Moon (1983:320) argues that underdeveloped states are more affected by external forces than are other members of the international system. Provided that international variables have important effects upon states, then studying this problem should be illustrative. Beyond this, investigating foreign investment serves as a means for ascertaining both the nature of the structure of the international system and the degree to which one of the supposedly most powerful actors in the contemporary international arena serves as a challenger to the state in the Third World. If international corporations are indeed modern leviathans, then this should be apparent most clearly in their relations with underdeveloped countries, which should be dominated decisively by international firms, for these states constitute the weakest contemporary institutional links in the modern Westphalian structure of sovereign independent units in international relations (see Morse, 1976:1–21, 23).

The purpose of this book is to explore systematically the effects upon underdeveloped countries of the direct foreign investments made by multinational corporations. As McGowan and Smith (1978:184) and Ray (1973:11) state, the bewildering array of claims and counterclaims regarding multinational corporations points to the need for thorough research. Much of the current literature on foreign investment reflects sentiment instead of careful analysis and is more an exercise in polemics and rhetorical excess than the product of careful reasoning. A basic goal herein is to examine the statements made about the effects of foreign investments with an eye to ascertaining whether they are logically consistent and theoretically plausible and whether they are supported by the available evidence.

While pursuing this goal, this analysis seeks to build upon and extend the systematic research conducted by other scholars. As Bornschier and Chase-Dunn (1985:xi) discuss, the disagreements regarding foreign investment have led to a growing number of empirical studies. One characteristic of these research efforts is that they focus almost exclusively upon the effects of foreign investment on economic growth and social distribution (see Bornschier et al., 1978:653–70; Rothgeb, 1984–85:3–10). Even though multinational corporations are regarded by most authors as having important, and perhaps profound, effects upon the foreign and domestic policies of host states, there is, as Leonard (1980:455) points out, a dearth of systematic research addressing these consequences. Thus, there is a basic need for research that investigates empirically the implications of foreign investment for politics and policy, as well as for economic processes, in poor countries. This book is the result of such research.

In conducting empirical research, the goal is to move beyond the often-found practice in the empirical literature of testing hypotheses in a general manner and speculating as to the exact mechanisms that may have produced any relationships found. Instead, an attempt is made to meet the standard Bueno de Mesquita (1985:122) sets for empirical analysis: the establishment of a superior explanation that accounts precisely for the behavior observed. This is done in two ways. At the conceptual level, the development of such an explanation is based upon considering the association between the multinational corporation and the underdeveloped host state as involving a contest between competing actors. In other words, the relationship shall be regarded as political, and political considerations pertaining to the differing strengths of the actors in the relationship and how they use the advantages they derive from their power shall be treated as fundamental for determining the probable effects of foreign investment, even when the effects under consideration are economic in nature. All too often, past analysis of the impacts of foreign investment upon Third World states has failed to consider the political context in which these effects occur. It is maintained here that pondering this political context carefully and using a framework built around concepts found in the literature on asymmetrical interdependence will yield fruitful results.

At a second level, greater precision is attained through the use of a more exact analytical design. For one thing, this research shall examine the sectoral location of foreign investments in the host economy. For the most part, past empirical research has based the discussion and measurement of foreign investment on total investments and has failed to take sectoral location into account. Rothgeb (1984a; 1984b; 1984–85; 1986a; 1986b) has demonstrated, however, that sectoral location is of fundamental theoretical and empirical importance for analyzing the effects of foreign investment. Hence, sectoral location is accounted for herein.

In addition to this, time-lagged analysis is employed. Many of the arguments about the role of multinational corporations are built around the conception that its impact shifts over time (see Bornschier et al., 1978; Bornschier, 1981), yet, surprisingly enough, few studies employ time-lagged analysis to explore these changing effects. As will be discussed in more detail later, time lags are built into the research design used in this book.

The substantive analysis begins with the consideration of how foreign investments affect host state foreign policy. As will be illustrated, three basic types of effects are discussed in the literature: the first sees foreign investment as a mechanism for controlling host states, the second regards it as creating interdependence, and the third treats multinational corporations and their home governments as natural targets for the frustrations associated with underdevelopment. These views are built around differing conceptions of the structure of the international system and regard host state foreign policy as varying dramatically in response to a multinational corporate presence.

A second subject of concern centers around the domestic political and social effects of foreign investment. Here one finds four basic conceptions of the role played by foreign investment. One views foreign investors as dominating the local government and domestic politics. Another envisions multinational corporations as allying themselves with a local government that is committed to the pursuit of development. A third regards the operation of foreign firms as creating detrimental by-products that affect the social and political life in the host country. Finally, the fourth posits that foreign firms essentially are apolitical and seek to avoid too close an involvement in the local political process. Again, the specific impact of multinational corporations upon host state political and social problems and policies differs substantially from one school of thought to another.

In the final substantive chapter, the concern shifts to economic growth. The implications for growth of the four conceptions relating foreign investment to domestic politics are considered, as are the specific paths of association between foreign investment and growth. Among the paths of association investigated are those that regard multinational firms as affecting growth via their effects on such things as capital availability, the degree to which the government plays a leading role in managing society, and changes in the composition of the local labor force.

In each substantive chapter, the analysis will follow the same pattern. First the various schools of thought found in the research literature will be examined in a brief outline. In doing this, an attempt will be made to illustrate the lines of intellectual conflict that exist between differing approaches. The underlying assumptions of each point of view, and where they converge and diverge, will be discussed. Following this, an attempt is made to develop a revised theoretical structure to explain the phenomenon of interest that both draws upon previous research and considers the effects of the political contest between the foreign firm and the host government. The specific relationships projected by this structure, together with the various expectations discussed in the differing schools of thought in the literature review, then will be analyzed empirically.

The preliminary projection is that multinational corporations will have effects on underdeveloped societies that vary according to the type of activity examined, the sectoral location of the investment, the level of development of the host state, and the time frame that one investigates. For example, it is suspected that while foreign investments may have the capacity for promoting growth, especially in very poor countries, these capabilities will only be used to a limited extent, leading to restricted benefits for the host state. In a similar fashion, it is anticipated that, depending upon the level of development and degree of dependence of the host state, foreign investments will contribute both to a greater degree of political and social conflict and to the implementation of more social reform. In other words, the expectation is that the analysis will reveal that multinational corporations are important actors with significant political, social, and economic effects on Third World states, but that they are far from the dominant force that some authors describe.

NOTES

1. See Nye and Keohane (1971a:ix-xxix; 1971:371–98) for a thorough discussion of the characteristics and importance of new actors, and the implications that the emergence of these actors has for international relations.

2. Some authors, such as Barnet and Muller (1974:17–18), reject the term *multinational corporation* as inaccurate, referring instead to global corporations, world corporations, or transnational corporations. While these authors make good points in explaining their choice of terminology, *multinational corporation* is used in this book because it has gained the widest use.

3. It should be noted that the figures for the largest and smallest Third World states are based upon the 84 states in the data set used for the analysis conducted in this book and are not based upon data for all Third World states. Using these data has no effect upon the figures for the largest states, all of which are represented in the data set. It does, however, bias the figures for the smallest states because some of the very smallest states are not in the data set. Hence, the disparity between the resources of multinational corporations and those of small underdeveloped states may be understated by the figures reported.

2

Foreign Investment and Foreign Policy

One of the most fundamental controversies surrounding the operations of multinational corporations in the Third World pertains to whether they are agents for creating and/or maintaining an international class structure that perpetuates a dominant role for industrialized core countries and a subordinate role for underdeveloped periphery countries. A key to understanding this dispute is the fact that the overwhelming majority of all direct foreign investments in underdeveloped countries are products of the activities of firms with ties of national origin to advanced core states. When this fact is juxtaposed with the dominant position played by industrial states in the international political and economic systems and with the fact that direct investments result in foreign ownership and control over some of the resources and productive capacity found in the host country, it is perhaps only natural that an important question of concern would revolve around whether corporate expansion serves to project home country influence into the Third World. Wells (1971:98) observes the "speculation that multinational enterprise based in the United States (or in any other industrial home country) is simply an extension of American culture and political interests abroad." Keohane and Ooms (1972:115), Vernon (1977:145), Moran (1978:95), and Kindleberger (1979:92) note that such conjecture leads many to expect a large foreign presence to have a strong effect upon the foreign policies of the host government toward the home state.

Although there is considerable discussion of the relationship between foreign investment and foreign policy, there is little agreement as to the nature of the effects of the former upon the latter. A perusal of the literature reveals the three basic conceptions of how the two are related, as mentioned in the introduction. The first, labeled the Trojan Horse model, regards multinational corporations as akin to the legendary wooden figure that was used to penetrate the ancient walled fortress in order to capture from within. The second, referred to as the Scapegoat model, perceives governments in underdeveloped countries as using foreign investors and their home states as targets to blame for the social and economic ills found in the host society. The final conception, the non–Foreign Entity model, regards foreign investors as seeking to hide their foreign origins and as having little effect upon foreign policy, except insofar as they create interdependence between the home and host countries.

These different points of view reflect the considerable conceptual confusion found in the literature. This confusion has been alleviated little by the cross-national research to date, for with the exception of Richardson (1978), scholars generally have not concerned themselves with these questions. Excellent case studies have been conducted by Pinelo (1973), Moran (1974), Sklar (1975), Evans (1979), and Fleet (1982) that illustrate some of the possible foreign policy consequences of foreign investment in Peru, Chile, Zambia, Brazil, and Colombia; however, as Przeworski and Teune (1970:4–8), McGowan (1975:56), and Bueno de Mesquita (1985:123–27) note, while case studies are useful, comparative research examining larger numbers of cases is required to understand a phenomenon more completely and to move toward greater theoretical development.

The purpose of this chapter is to examine the effect of direct foreign investment upon the foreign policy behavior of underdeveloped states.[1] In particular, the focus is upon the pattern of cooperation and conflict that Third World governments display toward the developed country that serves as the home state for the highest proportion of their total stock of foreign investments.[2] In other words, attention is centered upon how a larger foreign presence from a single foreign national source affects host government behavior toward that source. A key assumption in this chapter is that if the multinational corporation does create or maintain the international structure of control mentioned above, then it will be reflected in the foreign policy behavior of the host country.

The basic goals in this chapter are (1) to outline briefly the three conceptions just cited; (2) to point to divergences in underlying assumptions; (3) to suggest the specific conditions under which each may be plausible, the types of foreign policy behavior that should result, and how this behavior may change over time; and (4) to analyze these expectations systematically using cross-national research techniques. In pursuing these goals, this research seeks to expand upon Richardson's (1978) work, which examines the effect of foreign investment on one type of cooperation, voting compliance in the United Nations' General Assembly by countries dominated by the United States.

FOREIGN POLICY AND INVESTMENT PENETRATION

Trojan Horse

The Trojan Horse model is based upon an intellectual tradition that, as Vernon (1977:143) discusses, regards foreign investments as key mechanisms of imperialism. A summary of this conception should begin by noting that the underlying logic of this framework often varies subtly from author to author. A lengthy discussion of these differences is beyond the scope of the present effort.[3] The one overarching point of agreement among analysts taking this point of view is that foreign investments are used to control the host state.

According to this approach, a high level of foreign investments creates what Bodenheimer (1971:162) refers to as the "infrastructure of dependence," where the host state loses its ability to take independent action. This happens for several reasons. One is that foreigners gain control of the commanding heights of the host economy (Sunkel, 1979:221). When this happens, the key decisions regarding the host economy are made abroad, robbing the host of the ability to chart its own course (Dos Santos, 1971:226). Economic growth and development depend upon foreign behavior and foreign inputs (Bodenheimer, 1971:162; Cardoso and Faletto, 1979:162–63). Under these circumstances, the host government is forced to follow closely the policy preferences of foreigners. As Bodenheimer (1971:158) states, "Dependency means . . . that the alternatives open to the dependent nation are defined and limited by its integration into and functions within the world market."

Beyond this, Mahler (1981:272) notes that many analysts see a large foreign presence as creating a foreign-dominated elite in the host society. Galtung (1971:83–85) illustrates this with his center/periphery model. According to this model, the pattern of control by dominant, or center, states over underdeveloped, or peripheral, countries is both an *inter*national and an *intra*national phenomenon. Control occurs because the elite, or center, in the center nation (C in C) establishes a bridgehead into the periphery. This bridgehead is the local elite, or center (C in P). Hveem (1973:328) and Magdoff (1969:15) regard the multinational corporation as the central agent for establishing this pattern of hegemony. Senghaas (1975:257) concurs, stating that "today, the multinational corporations, centrally located in the different capitalist metropoles (center states) but operating globally, are the principle agents of this dynamics." Many other analysts agree.

Within this relationship, a harmony of interests is established between the C in C and the C in P, and a disharmony of interests exists between the C in P and the masses in the periphery. The harmony of interests is based on the one hand on the C in C's reliance upon the assistance of the C in P for the exploitation of the resources and for access to the markets and cheap labor found in the periphery, and on the other hand on the C in P's need for the aid of the C in C in order to maintain its dominant position and to gain access to the goods and privileges available from the center state. Thus, the C in P acts as an agent of the C in C, following its policy preferences in exchange for favors. Control is indirect and is based on the need of the C in P for the C in C. As Baran (1957:198) explains, the multinational corporation

uses its tremendous power to prop up the backward area's comprador administration, to disrupt and corrupt the social and political movements that oppose them, and to overthrow whatever progressive governments may rise to power and refuse to do the bidding of their imperialist overlords.

When this pattern of mastery occurs within a feudal structure, with a periphery state being dominated by a single center nation, then control is more pronounced (Galtung, 1971:89–90). Domination by a single center state greatly restricts periphery states and heightens their dependence because their elites are left with only a single source of external support (Chase-Dunn, 1978:174; Rubinson, 1977:22–23). A. G. Frank (1969:6–7) describes the result as an ''exploitative relationship (that) serves the interests of the metropoles which take advantage of this . . . structure.''

The implications for the foreign policy behavior of periphery states are profound. A high level of foreign penetration makes it impossible to pursue policies that are at variance with the desires of the dominant center state (Baran, 1957:196; Bodenheimer, 1971:170; Magdoff, 1969:37). All facets of foreign policy behavior are affected. Penetrated states must corporate and voice support for all diplomatic initiatives of the dominant state. In addition, they must cooperate economically, negotiating agreements, opening up their economies to exploitation, and turning to the center state for technical and other advice. Security policy also will focus on the dominant state, with the periphery nation agreeing to provide the hegemon with military bases, to purchase its weapons, to consummate alliances, and to extend to it any other privileges that it demands (Galtung, 1971:90–91). In effect, the dependent state becomes a consumer of the policy preferences of the dominant state and must cooperate and conform to its desires, while avoiding any form of conflictual behavior.

Scapegoat

Authors who discuss scapegoating often begin by noting the tremendous problems confronting the governments of underdeveloped countries. Such governments are confronted with immense burdens, for among other things they must build a national consciousness among their people, produce confidence in the government and increase its authority, create new social institutions, and transform the economy. Confounding these tasks is the intractable problem of poverty. Under such circumstances, these governments need to rally the people by giving them symbols that they can work *for* and, sometimes, *against*. At the same time, the government may seek to retain its own credibility and authority by placing the blame for failures on another object or institution. Attempting to rally the masses by presenting them with a symbol that is accused of being responsible for social ills is the essence of scapegoating, as the term is used by most authors who discuss the phenomenon in connection with foreign investment.[4]

Within underdeveloped countries, multinational corporations often are the focus of considerable frustration and hostility and are credible targets for blame. Their foreign origins make them suspect. In fact, host governments frequently perceive foreign investors as actual or potential agents of their home governments. This perception inclines host government officials to take a skeptical, and often hostile, view of corporate activities (Sklar, 1975:183). The firm may be seen as working closely with its home government and as having the automatic support of the home government whenever it clashes with the host government (Ranis, 1976:105; Vernon, 1971:235–36; 1977:146). In addition, the corporation is regarded as introducing foreign values into the host society, thus undermining local culture and creating a host of social problems (I. Frank, 1980:28–29); Vernon, 1977:14–15). Foreign films also may antagonize the traditional elite in the host society, for the firm may be perceived as a competitor that introduces types of business practices and labor policies that threaten the prominent position hitherto enjoyed by this elite (Pinelo, 1973:12–13, 39, 57). Moreover, as I. Frank (1980:28–29) notes, not only is the corporation foreign, but it is also private, representing a system of commerce that is alien to most poor countries and that is associated by many with the excesses of imperialism. Barnet and Muller (1974:193), Moran (1978:93–94), Pinelo (1973:35, 92), Richardson (1978:84), and Vernon (1971:53) all argue that these factors incline underdeveloped hosts to resort to scapegoating at the expense of the corporation to relieve frustration, to distance themselves from the responsibility for social ills, and to rally the people against an imperialist target.

To the degree that the firm is perceived as an agent of its home government, this frustration may be expected to spill over and affect the foreign policy behavior of the host government toward the home state. Diaz-Alejandro (1970:329) sees this perception as strongly reinforced by an increasingly greater dependence upon investments from a single foreign national source. When this is the case, the probability increases that the host government will regard itself as not just dealing with corporations on an individual basis, but as confronting a significant *national* presence from another (developed) country. In this situation, it is more likely that the host government will view this presence as imperialist and will seek to use the foreign government as a symbol for rallying and mobilizing its people.

The result should be foreign policy behavior reflecting hostility toward the foreign investor's home country. The specific type of conflict and the conditions under which it may occur are discussed below.

Non–Foreign Entity

As noted above, the Trojan Horse conception is based upon the view that the multinational corporation is an instrument used for controlling underdeveloped countries. The non–Foreign Entity model is built upon a very different foundation. To begin with, foreign investors are seen as unable to rely upon the support of their home governments. Staley (1979:189) argues that foreign investors and their home governments often have conflicting desires and that when the wishes of investors run counter to those of the home government, the investors receive "hesitant or grudging support, no support at all, or active opposition." Barnet and Muller (1974:75–76) and Vernon (1977:184) concur.

Moreover, Vernon (1971:6) depicts multinational corporations as competing with one another for market shares and resources in the host state, creating an atmosphere in which firms often refuse to support one another in conflicts with the host government. Thus, foreign investors are not a monolithic bloc seeking to dominate the underdeveloped host, even when they share the same national origins (Moran, 1978:93–94).

Beyond this, Leonard (1980:469) and Pinelo (1973:xiii) state that host governments are not as easily dominated as some authors maintain and that they are especially wary of foreign investors. Indeed, I. Frank (1980:41) mentions that this wariness significantly increases the difficulties confronting foreign investors who do wish to influence governmental policy.

As a result of these considerations, Keohane and Ooms (1972:110) conclude that multinational corporations make an effort to avoid the appearance of being involved in local politics for fear that to do otherwise might provoke a xenophobic backlash. Such a backlash would serve only to undermine the primary goal of the corporation: to engage in business in order to secure a profit. In order to avoid these difficulties, Vernon (1976:47) suggests that foreign investors regard it as a sound practice "to remain as unobtrusive as possible in the local economy." Hence, foreign corporations seek to hide their foreign origins, appearing "either as a local corporation or as a vague world entity." (Barnet and Muller, 1974:90). In doing so, the corporation behaves as a national firm and tries to create the impression that it is loyal to the host government (Barnet and Muller, 1974:16; I. Frank, 1980:61; Sklar, 1975:183; Wells, 1971:102).

Such corporate behavior may have one of two possible effects on foreign policy behavior. The first is that multinational corporations are so successful in hiding their national origins, behaving as local businesses, and staying out of local politics that they do not affect foreign policy behavior. This is the null variation of the non–Foreign Entity model.

The second possibility is that even though foreign corporations seek to disguise their national origins and attempt to steer clear of politics, a large stock of foreign investment creates strong economic linkages and interdependence between the host and home states that affect foreign policy behavior. Keohane and Nye (1977:10–14), Polachek (1980:59–61), and Richardson (1976:1098) discuss economic linkages as among the strongest ties that bind states to one another and affect foreign policy, and Vernon (1976:41) sees the multinational corporation as a key agent for promoting interdependence.

The implications of the above possibilities are discussed in the following pages.

REFINING THE MODELS

In assessing the above models, it is useful to begin by noting a fundamental point of agreement. Each conception is built around the twin assumptions that an asymmetrical relationship exists between advanced industrialized states and underdeveloped countries, with the former being far stronger than the latter, and that the foreign policy behavior of underdeveloped countries toward developed countries will reflect this asymmetry. The divergence among the three schools of thought appears when they consider how developed states use their strength and the sort of role the multinational corporation plays in this asymmetrical relationship. Within the Trojan Horse framework, developed states are seen as establishing an international structure of control and the multinational corporation is regarded as an active agent of its home government, working closely with that government (with which it has a virtual identity of interests) to establish a firm grip on underdeveloped countries to guarantee a continuing access to cheap raw materials, inexpensive labor, and markets.

The Scapegoat and non–Foreign Entity conceptions are built around a much different point of view. Scholars discussing these phenomena see the multinational corporation as acting on behalf of its own interests, which very often do not coincide with those of its home government. Nevertheless, foreign investment affects foreign policy behavior toward the foreign investor's home country because the host government *perceives* the foreign presence as creating important linkages to the home country. Scapegoating occurs when these ties are perceived as leading to too great a role for foreigners in the host country and as creating local problems. An interdependent pattern of behavior is found when host officials perceive these linkages as creating the need for special contacts with the home country in order to secure certain much-needed benefits.

In sorting through these views, one may begin by considering the basic nature of an asymmetrical relationship. Dolan et al. (1982:389) posit that asymmetry is a product of two factors: (1) the resources available to each actor and (2) the intensity of involvement that each partner has in the relationship. The more intensely involved state with fewer resources will be more dependent (see Waltz, 1970:207).

This is the type of situation confronting underdeveloped countries. Their lower level of development results in fewer available resources. Such especially in the case with countries that are very poor and least developed, for such societies simply do not possess the capital, modern technology, and entrepreneurial talent to tap efficiently such potential resources as they may have within their borders (Barnet and Muller, 1974:133–47; Vernon, 1977:139–75; Rothgeb, 1986a:126). A low level of development also heightens intensity of involvement by producing a desire for rapid progress, which many leaders in the Third World see as requiring both ongoing and long-term contacts with industrialized states. The result is a greater degree of sensitivity and vulnerability for the underdeveloped, or subordinate, country to the behavior of its developed, or dominant, partner. Sensitivity refers to the short-term costs that an actor must pay because of its partner's behavior, and vulnerability relates to the ability of an actor to reduce these costs over the long run by adopting new policies (Keohane and Nye, 1977:12–13). A high stock of foreign investment from the dominant partner increases intensity of involvement and magnifies dependence, for it gives foreigners control over a substantial proportion of the host state's resources and productive capacity (Armstrong, 1981:402).

In addition to the conditions that produce asymmetry, one should consider the factors that motivate decision makers in subordinate countries. Dolan et al. (1982:391–92) suggest that two key considerations for such leaders are the economic well-being of their society and its autonomy. Regarding economic well-being as a basic goal assumes that governments prefer that their societies be as prosperous as possible. Treating autonomy as a goal assumes that governments prefer independence of action and seek to avoid domination.

Scholars who work within the Trojan Horse framework envision a situation in which the autonomy of subordinate countries in an asymmetrical relationship is restricted severely. The mechanics of the operation of the international structure of control work to suppress the desire for independence, allowing the dominant state, working hand in hand with its agent, the multinational corporation, to impose its will on the subordinate country to such an extent that subordinate country foreign policy behavior will reflect the preferences of the dominant state. As Bodenheimer (1971:170) puts it when writing of Latin America, "The autonomy of Latin American decision-makers is not to be taken for granted; while they may go through the motions of deciding policy, the substance of their decisions often reflects foreign interests."

This situation is made possible both because of the tremendous strength of the hegemon in relation to the underdeveloped host and because of the payoffs (in the form of bribes and so forth) that are made to the local elite. It is assumed that foreign investors establish and maintain a pattern of control whereby they provide enhanced economic well-being to a small segment of the local population and that one of the costs paid for these benefits is a surrender, either explicit or implicit, of foreign policy autonomy. In effect, "multinational corporations . . . *de*nationalize [emphasis in the original] a section of the native bourgeoisies in the countries they penetrate." (Magdoff and Sweezy, 1971:97).

Hence, if the multinational corporation acts as an instrument of control, a Trojan Horse pattern of asymmetrical domination should be most apparent when three conditions exist: (1) the host country is very weak and is among the least developed members of the Third World, (2) there is a high stock of foreign investment, and (3) these investments are overwhelmingly from a single foreign national source. The first condition is necessary because it results in the greatest degree of discrepancy in strength within the asymmetrical relationship. One may assume that the yielding of foreign policy autonomy that is implicit in the Trojan Horse model would only occur when the host country is least able to do otherwise. The findings of Armstrong (1981), Richardson (1976), and Richardson and Kegley (1980) buttress this assumption, for it was found that cooperation with the hegemonic state in an asymmetrical relationship was only given grudgingly, apparently because subordinate country decision makers sought to avoid domination. When the host country is at a very low level of development, and therefore is weak, it becomes difficult to balk at domination.

The second condition is necessary because it creates a high degree of foreign penetration and a large role for foreigners in the host economy. The final condition is necessary because it contributes to the feudal arrangement noted above that restricts the host elite to a single source of foreign support.

Given these necessary conditions, one may point to a key problem with the logic of the Trojan Horse conception. This is that the countries that are most easily controlled do not match well with some of the goals of domination. As discussed above, the goals of such economic mastery are access to markets, inexpensive labor, and cheap raw materials, while the most likely candidates for control are the least developed members of the Third World. Rothgeb (1986a:129) points out, however, that the very poverty of extremely poor countries makes them inferior markets and sources of labor. Consequently, if a Trojan Horse pattern of domination does exist, then it is probable that it pertains to the exploitation of raw materials in the poorest members of the Third World. Magdoff (1969:195) and Rubinson (1976:642) support this line of argument, maintaining that ensuring access to cheap raw materials is the primary reason for multinational domination of poor countries.

Thus, very poor countries with a higher stock of foreign investment in mining that is predominantly from one foreign national source should be most inclined toward the display of foreign policy behavior that is described in the literature. Such behavior would include greater cooperation of all types with the hegemon and less conflict. Moreover, as Moon (1983:333) notes, since one is assuming such complete domination, this pattern should not vary over time.

A very different set of conclusions emerges when one considers the relationships that may be expected within the non–Foreign Entity and Scapegoat frameworks. Both of these conceptions operate from the premise that while the multinational corporation may play an important role in underdeveloped countries, it does not create and maintain conditions that rob the host government of its freedom of action in the foreign policy arena. This does not mean that foreign investment has no impact on foreign policy, for it does. These effects, however, are the product of the interdependent linkages that foreign investment fosters between the home and host countries and may be expected to vary according to the sectoral location of the investment, the level of development of the host country, and the passage of time.

Illustrating these points requires that one consider the nature of the interdependence that foreign investment may create. As discussed above, the differences in resource availability and intensity of involvement between the developed home state and the underdeveloped host country leads to asymmetry. For the host state, asymmetry contributes to a greater sensitivity and vulnerability that is heightened by a large stock of foreign investment (Richardson, 1976:1098–99; 1978:14). Rothgeb (1986a) points out that the nature of the sensitivity and vulnerability produced by foreign investment varies according to the sectoral location of the investment. In particular, manufacturing and mining investments have different effects. On the one hand, investments in both sectors lead to sensitivity; manufacturing investments do so by creating a reliance on inputs from the home state for capital, technology, and management talent, while mining investments lead to a dependence by the host state upon the marketing structures for raw materials found in the home country (see Vernon, 1971:56; Pinelo, 1973:54). On the other hand, the vulnerability resulting from these investments differs. A large manufacturing presence may be perceived by host government officials as requiring a complex and not easily replaced ongoing foreign contribution (see Vernon, 1977:10–11; Frieden, 1981:407–13), while mining enterprises are regarded as relatively uncomplicated, and foreigners are seen as replaceable (Vernon, 1971:26–59; Moran, 1974).

Thus, one might expect that early on each type of investment will receive a favorable reception by host officials, as they perceive the investments as contributing to the economic well-being of their societies. Mining investments may be seen as doing so by helping to tap previously unreachable resources (Diaz-Alejandro, 1970:322; Vernon, 1971:45–47; Heilbroner, 1963:110–11), and manufacturing by bringing much needed capital, technology, and entrepreneurial talent. As times passes, and the sensitivity of the host state becomes increasingly apparent, the concern with autonomy should become greater (Reuber, 1973:17). Safeguarding autonomy should require that the role of foreigners be limited. The immediate economic well-being of the host society, however, may run counter to this requirement, for there is a need for the manufacturing inputs and/or access to markets that are available only from the home country. Hence, these needs must be balanced with one another. This may be accomplished by gearing foreign policy toward restricting further economic, technical, and cultural penetration from the home country, thereby limiting the expansion of the parameters of the foreign role in the host society and protecting freedom of action. At the same time, the degree of diplomatic and verbal cooperation with the home state may be increased to preserve an air of amiability in relations, thereby maintaining the economic well-being stemming from the association. In effect, foreign policy is designed to sustain existing relations, while at the same time preventing the possible loss of autonomy that might result from an extension.

When foreign policy behavior involves scapegoating, it may be regarded as an outgrowth of the belief that the foreign presence makes only a minimal contribution to local economic well-being, while at the same time severely threatening local autonomy. The result should be a considerable degree of frustration. In such circumstances, the behavior associated with pursuing the goals of economic well-being and autonomy no longer pull in opposite directions, and there is little incentive for the host state to display any form of cooperation, no matter how minor, while the inclination toward conflict designed to reduce the foreign role in the host economy should increase substantially. As long as foreign investment is perceived as helping the local economy, there is scant reason to expect scapegoating, because there are benefits gained from refraining from such behavior. When these benefits are perceived as no longer existing, then the temptation toward using the foreign presence for political advantage should be magnified.

These beliefs regarding the effects of foreign investment should only evolve under certain conditions: (1) the perceived vulnerability of the host state to the investors and their home country must be low, (2) the investment must be regarded as exploitative and as contributing little to local development efforts, (3) the investment should stand out as a highly visible example of a foreign presence, (4) the investors must appear to have close ties to their home countries, and (5) as was mentioned above, the investments should be overwhelmingly from a single foreign national source. The first condition reduces the perception that the economic well-being of the host country will be affected by scapegoating, the second and third provide a basis for regarding foreigners as the root of local troubles, and the fourth and fifth furnish reasons for the resentment to spill over to affect foreign policy behavior toward the home country.

The first four of these conditions are associated with foreign investments in mining. As was discussed previously, over the long run host officials are likely to regard the vulnerability stemming from investments in the mining sector as low, while the vulnerability associated with manufacturing investments may appear high.[5] Pinelo (1973:12–13), Vernon (1977:149), and Mahler (1981:273) point out that mining investments are seen as exploitative because they remove local resources for what appears to be meager compensation. Resource extraction projects also are highly visible because they tend to concentrate in small enclaves, or company towns, near the site where the mining takes place and they stand out as islands of relative wealth in a sea of poverty (Mahler, 1981:273; Pinelo, 1973;12–13; Sklar, 1975:25; Vernon, 1971:196). Finally, Reuber (1973:228) reports that mining enterprises are very closely tied to their parent firms in the home country, and Wells (1971:107) states that they make little effort to hide these foreign ties.

Thus, scapegoating in foreign policy should center on the home country of mining investors when the investments are predominantly from a single foreign national source. Over the long run, the cost of striking out at the investor's home country may be perceived as small and the benefits as substantial. As Adorno et al. (1969:223, 485) argue, these are the types of conditions under which scapegoating occurs.

The specific behavior associated with scapegoating should be designed to serve the complementary purposes of reducing the role foreigners play in the host society while also providing a highly visible symbol to the people that action is being taken to deal with those who are to blame for local problems. This may be accomplished through conflict with the home country that involves such things as terminating economic agreements, expelling foreign technical advisors, closing embassies, and recalling diplomats. More violent conflict should be avoided, however, for the risks would be disproportionate to the potential gains.

The patterns associated with interdependence and scapegoating in foreign policy behavior should be prevalent among countries that are most susceptible to foreign domination. Such countries are those that are highly dependent, that is, very poor countries with a high stock of investment from a single foreign national source. In this type of country the initial expectations regarding the benefits to be derived from foreign investment should be high, the attachment to the vestiges of independence strong, and the social and economic problems great. Thus, later disillusionment and frustration should be correspondingly high. The result should be a situation in which foreign investment initially is greeted with enthusiasm and cooperation, followed by a mounting concern with independence accompanied by a desire to preserve benefits, and finally by growing frustration as social and economic problems persist.

In more developed countries, a different pattern should exist. Evans (1979) provides clues as to why this is the case. One reason is that the greater resource availability in more developed societies makes domination by foreigners a more difficult task and the consequent threat to autonomy less pronounced, and it also places the host society in a more favorable position for regulating foreign investors' behavior. Another is that foreign investment, especially in the manufacturing sector, plays a much more subtle role in such societies, often working closely with host officials in a mutually beneficial arrangement. Under these conditions, the perceived need to use foreign policy to protect one's independence is not as pressing, for the foreigners will be regarded as controllable. Moreover, the ability of the multinational corporation to fit in as a non–foreign entity is greater when it is a part of this type of an arrangement.

SUMMARY

The foregoing discussion outlines three views of how foreign investment affects foreign policy behavior in Third World countries. Each conception is based upon the belief that there is an asymmetrical relationship between the advanced industrialized home countries of the foreign investors and the underdeveloped host state. The views part company over whether a large foreign investment presence results in a loss of autonomy for the host country. The Trojan Horse conception is built around the assumption that autonomy is lost; the Scapegoat and non–Foreign Entity frameworks rest upon the assumption that it is not.

These varying assumptions regarding autonomy contribute to different projections regarding the foreign policy behavior of the host. It is expected that if the Trojan Horse model is accurate, then, among host countries that are very poor and where the foreign investments are predominantly from a single foreign national source, the stock of foreign investment in mining will be positively related to displays of cooperation and negatively related to acts of conflict with the hegemonic state. This pattern of relationships should not vary over time.

The non–Foreign Entity and Scapegoat conceptions also project that the impact of foreign investments upon foreign policy should be found among extremely poor countries with investments from a single foreign national source. The hypothesized effects, however, are different and vary both according to the sectoral location of the investment and with the passage of time. In mining, the total stock of investments should be

1. positively related both to verbal diplomatic and to economic, technical, and cultural cooperation with the investor's home country over the short run,
2. negatively related to economic, technical, and cultural cooperation and positively related to verbal cooperation after a short time lag, and
3. positively related to economic, technical, and cultural conflict over the long run.

In manufacturing, the total stock of investments should be

1. positively related both to verbal diplomatic and to economic, technical, and cultural cooperation over the short run and
2. negatively related to economic, technical, and cultural cooperation and positively related to verbal cooperation both after a short time lag and over the long run.

Before turning to the empirical analysis, a final point should be made. This concerns the controls required when investigating the above hypotheses in order to avoid the problem of spurious relationships. A key force that was discussed as affecting the host state's foreign policy behavior was its resource availability. Controlling for this factor requires that two types of variables be included in the analysis in this chapter: (1) the resources available domestically and (2) those that come from external sources. The latter variable may be especially important within the present context, for the ability to acquire resources internationally may have a strong effect upon a state's orientation toward the international arena and therefore upon its foreign policy behavior. Measures for each of these variables are included in the following analysis.

THE RESEARCH DESIGN

The hypotheses in this chapter are investigated with a cross-national design. The same basic design, drawing upon the same sample of countries, is used throughout this book. Data were gathered for 84 countries classified by the World Bank (1976, 1980) as underdeveloped. Problems of data availability precluded the analysis of a larger sample of states.[6] States classified by the Organization for Economic Cooperation and Development (OECD) as offshore banking centers or by the World Bank as capital exporters were not included in the sample. Offshore banking centers were omitted because, as Rothgeb (1984b:1066) notes, the offshore activities greatly inflate foreign investment scores. The exclusion of capital exporting states is suggested by Jackman (1982:192). The nations included in the data set are listed in Appendix 1.

The dependent variable in this chapter is the foreign policy behavior displayed by underdeveloped host states toward the largest foreign national source of their foreign investments in the mining and manufacturing sectors. Testing the hypotheses in this chapter required the examination of several types of foreign policy cooperation and conflict: (1) verbal expressions of cooperation; (2) economic, technical, and cultural cooperation; (3) military and security cooperation; (4) verbal expressions of conflict; and (5) economic, technical, and cultural acts of conflict.[7]

These categories of cooperation and conflict were measured using data from the Conflict and Peace Data Bank (COPDAB) international scale.[8] The COPDAB files contain events data for a sample of 135 countries for the years 1948–78. The COPDAB international scale codes the foreign policy behavior that each of these 135 states, or actors, directs toward the other states, or targets, that are found in the international system. Each action is coded on a scale that seeks to capture the type and degree of cooperation or conflict displayed (see Azar, 1980:143–52; 1982:25–29). Values 1 through 3 on this scale represent various types of military and security cooperation, including establishing military alliances, waging war as allies, training military personnel, and granting military aid. Values 4 and 5 represent such economic, technical, and cultural cooperation as negotiating and establishing economic treaties, setting up joint scientific or technical committees, opening diplomatic relations, sending or receiving economic or technical advisors, granting or receiving economic aid or loans, and beginning cultural exchanges. Values 6 and 7 represent verbal cooperation, such as statements of support for the foreign policy of the target and issuing a joint policy communiqué indicating agreement with the target. Values 9 and 10 include verbal conflict, such as objections to the target's foreign policy and accusing the target of having malevolent intentions. Finally, values 11 and 12 include such economic, technical, and cultural conflict as terminating economic treaties, abolishing joint scientific or technical committees, breaking diplomatic relations, expelling foreign economic or technical advisors, cancelling economic aid or loans, and ending cultural exchanges. These points on the scale conform closely to the types of cooperation and conflict that must be measured for this study.

Proportions were used in calculating scores for the dependent variables, for, as Hoggard (1974:355–59) notes, the failure to do so leads to situations where states that have large total numbers of events, a phenomenon which is often a function of the news sources used to compile the data base, will have high scores, even though a small percentage of their total events may be of any particular type. Rothgeb (1982–83:48) recommends the use of proportions as a means for addressing these problems. Another consideration in calculating scores was that the values obtained reflect the degree to which the host nation's behavior toward the home state differs from its behavior toward all targets. A high proportion of any type of either cooperation or conflict directed toward the home state may not be especially significant if the host state directs the same type of behavior toward all of its targets. When the proportion of a particular form of behavior is far in excess of, or is far below, the proportion for all targets, then one has an indication that the home state is the object of special attention.

The cooperation and conflict scores were computed with these considerations in mind. The procedure used may be illustrated by considering how security cooperation scores were computed. Five steps were involved:

1. All actions for each actor that were coded as a 1, 2, or 3 on the COPDAB international scale were summed separately for each time period examined.

2. The figure from step 1 was divided by the total number of events that each actor had for each time period.

3. All actions for each actor that were coded as a 1, 2, or 3 on the COPDAB international scale and that were targeted by the largest foreign national source of investments were summed for each time period.

4. The figure from step 3 was divided by the total number of events targeted at the largest foreign national source of investments for each time period.

5. The figure from step 2 was subtracted from the figure from step 4.

An analogous procedure using the appropriate COPDAB international scale values was used to calculate each of the other cooperation and conflict scores. Separate scores were calculated to reflect each host state's foreign policy behavior toward its largest foreign national source in manufacturing and in mining.

Foreign policy behavior was conceptualized as a function either of the total stock of foreign investment in mining (abbreviated TotInvMin) or in manufacturing (TotInvMan) from the largest foreign national score. Two control variables also were included: (1) the total population of the host state in the first year of each time period (Pop), and (2) the total amount of long-term external public debt incurred during each time period (Debt). Total population was used to control for domestic resource availability (see Jackman, 1982:188). External public debt controlled for resources obtained externally (see Rothgeb, 1986a:134).[9]

Following the procedures of previous researchers (Jackman, 1982:187–88; Rothgeb, 1984b:1067; 1984–85:12), stock of foreign investment in manufacturing and mining and total external public debt were weighted respectively by total GDP from the manufacturing sector, total GDP from mining, and total GDP from all sectors. Total population was logarithmically transformed because it is skewed. Unless otherwise indicated, stocks of foreign investment were weighted in the analysis throughout this book using the same procedure. Logarithmic transformations also were employed for data with skewed distributions (as shall be noted in each case) whenever necessary. Constant 1970 United States dollar values were used in calculating all monetary values used in the analysis.[10] The sources used to obtain data for all of the variables used in this analysis are in Appendix 2.

The analysis required the examination of terms representing the interaction between stock of foreign investment in manufacturing and mining and (1) the level of development of the host state and (2) the proportion of total stocks in each of these sectors from the largest foreign national source. As shall be done in similar circumstances throughout this book, dummy variables were created to represent high and low levels of development. The variable for high development (HiDevel) was produced by assigning a value of 1 to all states with a GDP per capita equal to or greater than $400 per year and a value of 0 to states with a value less than $400. States with a value of 1 were regarded as more developed. The variable for low development (LoDevel) was constructed by assigning a value of 1 to all states with a GDP per capita less than or equal to $100 per year and a value of 0 to all states with a value greater than $100. States with a value of 1 were regarded as very poor. The variable representing a high proportion of investments from the largest foreign national source (HiConcen) was created by assigning a value of 1 to states where 70 percent or more of the investments were from the largest foreign source and a value of 0 to states where less than 70 percent were from the largest source.[11] Countries with a value of 1 were treated as having a high concentration of investments from one foreign national source. Separate high concentration variables were created for investments in mining and in manufacturing.

Interaction terms were calculated by multiplying the total stock of foreign investment in mining and in manufacturing from the largest foreign national source first by the dummy variable for low development and by the appropriate variable for high concentration and then by the dummy variable for high development and by the appropriate variable for high concentration. This yielded four terms representing the interaction between (1) stocks of investment in mining, low development, and high concentration; (2) stock in mining, high development, and high concentration; (3) stock in manufacturing, low development, and high concentration; and (4) stock in manufacturing, high development, and high concentration.

Standard multiple regression analysis was used to investigate the hypothesized relationships. Use of this technique allows one to examine the effect of the independent variable on the dependent variable while statistically controlling for other variables (Lewis-Beck, 1980:49–51). Scatterplots of the bivariate relationships between the independent and dependent variables were examined to check for nonlinear associations. No apparent patterns were found.[12] As suggested by Lewis-Beck (1980:60), the independent and control variables were regressed on one another to check for multicollinearity. Severe problems (R^2 greater than .90) were found for equations that included the interaction terms and the main effects of the dummy variables and of stocks of foreign investment. The solution to the problem was found by using separate regression equations to examine the effects of the interaction terms and of the variables used to create these terms.[13] It should be noted that the use of regression analysis, the examination of scatterplots, and the check for multicollinearity procedures are used in the analysis conducted in each chapter of this book.

An example of the regression models used may be illustrated by considering the analysis of the effects of manufacturing investments on security cooperation:

(1) Security Cooperation = $a + b1\text{TotInvMan} + b2\text{Pop} + b3\text{Debt} + e$

(2) Security Cooperation = $a + b1\text{LoDevel} \times \text{HiConcen} \times \text{TotInvMan} + b2\text{Pop} + b3\text{Debt} + e$

(3) Security Cooperation = $a + b1\text{HiDevel} \times \text{HiConcen} \times \text{TotInvMan} + b2\text{Pop} + b3\text{Debt} + e$

The same types of equations were used to investigate the other forms of foreign policy behavior. The models for examining the effects of mining investments were analogous, except that the relevant variables for mining were substituted for their manufacturing counterparts.

Both synchronic and time-lagged analysis were employed to test for the short- and long-term effects of foreign investment on foreign policy behavior. Synchronic analysis, in which the independent and dependent variables are measured at the same point in time, allows one to test for immediate relationships. Time lags allow one to examine the longer-term associations between the variables. Time lagging is accomplished by measuring the independent variables for one period and the dependent variable for a subsequent point (or points) in time. As McGowan (1975:66) notes, such analysis is useful for ascertaining causal direction, for causes must precede effects. Time lags of three, six, and nine years were investigated to determine the effects of the independent variables on the dependent variables in periods beginning three, six, and nine years after the time at which the independent variables were measured.

The periods examined were 1967–69, 1970–72, 1973–75, and 1976–78. The lack of information for total stock of foreign investment made it impossible to obtain data for years prior to 1967.[14] In addition, the COPDAB files only contain data through 1978. This problem of data availability for underdeveloped countries plagued data gathering for each of the chapters of this book. Three-year averages were examined where possible, for, as Weisskopf (1972:29) points out, figures for single years often reflect idiosyncracies.

The synchronic analysis involved measuring the independent and dependent variables for the 1967–69 period. The foreign investment data, the values for GDP per capita, and the total population figures used were for 1967. External public debt and the foreign policy behavior variables were measured for 1967–69. For the time-lagged analysis, the foreign investment variables and GDP per capita were measured for 1967, while the dependent and control variables were measured for 1970–72 (three-year lag), 1973–75 (six-year lag), and 1976–78 (nine-year lag).

Prior to presenting the findings, it may be useful to state the patterns of results that were projected in the above theoretical discussion. It was hypothesized that if the Trojan Horse conception is correct, then the interaction among low development, high concentration, and total stocks in mining will be positively related to each of the measures of foreign policy cooperation and negatively associated with the measures of conflict with the largest foreign national source of mining investments. These results should be consistent over time.

Within the interdependence and scapegoating frameworks, a different situation is expected, for findings should vary both over time and according to the sectoral location of the investment. Foreign policy behavior toward the largest foreign national source of mining investments should follow a shifting pattern wherein the interaction among low development, high concentration, and stock in mining will be (1) positively related to economic and technical and to verbal diplomatic cooperation over the short run, (2) negatively related to economic and technical cooperation and positively related to verbal cooperation as time passes, and (3) positively related to economic and technical conflict over the long run. Foreign policy behavior toward the largest foreign national source of manufacturing investments should follow a course that is similar to that of mining, except that the long-term conflict should not occur. Instead, there should be a continuing pattern of a negative relationship for economic and technical cooperation and a positive association for verbal cooperation. The reader is reminded that the theoretical discussion pertaining to these frameworks indicated that foreign investment should have only these effects. Consequently, there should be no impact upon the other forms of foreign policy cooperation and conflict included in the analysis.

RESULTS

The results for mining investments are in Tables 2.1 through 2.4.[15] The synchronic results in Table 2.1 reveal no immediate effect by foreign investment upon foreign policy behavior. Table 2.2 shows that after a three-year time lag, there is a positive relationship between stocks in mining and economic and technical cooperation ($p < .05$, $R^2 = .16$). Following this, Table 2.3 illustrates that after six years the interaction among low development, high concentration, and stocks in mining is negatively related to economic and technical cooperation ($p < .001$, $R^2 = .33$) and positively associated with verbal cooperation ($p < .001$, $R^2 = .47$), and Table 2.4 indicates that after nine years, there is a positive relationship with economic and technical conflict ($p < .01$, $R^2 = .41$).

This arrangement of findings conforms well with the projections associated with the interdependence and scapegoating models. The types of cooperation and conflict displayed and the time sequencing is generally as was projected, as are the types of countries that are most affected. The only exception to this is the early pattern of cooperation. Instead of being limited to poor countries with a high concentration of investment from one foreign national source and extending both to economic and technical and to verbal diplomatic cooperation, the positive relationship found was general among all countries and pertained only to economic and technical cooperation. An explanation for this difference

Table 2.1
Synchronic Results for Cooperation and Conflict with the Largest Foreign National Source of Mining Investments

Dependent Variable	TotInvMin	LoDevel x HiConcen x TotInvMin	HiDevel x HiConcen x TotInvMin	Pop	Debt	R^2
Security	.27			.38*	.31	.16
Cooperation		-.19		.29	.29	.13
			.20	.34*	.29	.14
Economic and	.17			.09	.14	-.05
Technical		-.02		.04	.11	-.07
Cooperation			.09	.06	.12	-.07
Verbal	-.04			-.04	-.26	-.02
Cooperation		.03		-.03	-.25	-.02
			.00	-.03	-.25	-.02
Verbal	-.17			-.17	-.02	-.05
Conflict		.14		-.11	.00	-.06
			-.12	-.14	.00	-.06
Economic and	-.21			-.08	-.09	-.04
Technical		-.15		-.02	-.04	-.06
Conflict			-.13	-.05	-.07	-.07

Note: 37 is the sample size.
*p<.05

shall be discussed below. For the present, it should be noted that these findings provide little support for the Trojan Horse conception of how foreign investments affect host state foreign policy.

The results for manufacturing investments are in Tables 2.5 through 2.8. As was the case with mining investments, the synchronic results in Table 2.5 show no immediate effect on foreign policy cooperation and conflict. The three-year-lagged results in Table 2.6 reveal a positive relationship between the interaction of low development, high concentration, and stocks in manufacturing and verbal cooperation (p< .05, R^2 = .06). In Table 2.7, the six-year-lagged findings indicate that countries with low development, high concentration, and higher stocks in manufacturing display lower amounts of economic and technical cooperation (p< .001, R^2 = .18) and higher levels of verbal cooperation (p< .01, R^2 = .22). Finally, as shown in Table 2.8, after nine years stocks in manufacturing are negatively associated with economic and technical cooperation (p< .05, R^2 = .08) and are positively related to verbal cooperation (p< .01, R^2 = .15).

Once again, these findings follow the pattern that was projected in the interdependence hypotheses. The effects centered on poor countries that are more dependent, and the behavior displayed and the times at which it was displayed are as expected. There were only two variations from the interdependence hypotheses. The first was the lack of an early positive relationship with economic and technical cooperation. When this finding is considered together with the

Table 2.2

Three-Year Time-Lag Results for Cooperation and Conflict with the Largest Foreign National Source of Mining Investments

Dependent Variable	TotInvMin	LoDevel x HiConcen x TotInvMin	HiDevel x HiConcen x TotInvMin	Pop	Debt	R^2
Security	-.08			.11	-.06	-.06
Cooperation		-.11		.14	-.09	-.05
			-.03	.13	-.07	-.06
Economic and	.36*			.44**	-.01	.16
Technical		.02		.33	.02	.03
Cooperation			.16	.36*	.00	.06
Verbal	-.12			-.36*	-.02	.04
Cooperation		.15		-.32	-.01	.05
			-.06	-.33	-.02	.03
Verbal	-.08			-.07	-.09	-.07
Conflict		-.15		-.04	-.12	-.05
			.00	-.04	-.10	-.08
Economic and	-.26			.06	.16	.02
Technical		-.10		.14	.13	-.03
Conflict			-.15	.10	.16	-.02

Note: 38 is the sample size.
*p<.05
**p<.01

three-year-lagged result for mining investments, one finds that mining investments led to more economic and technical cooperation, but not to verbal cooperation, while the reverse was true for manufacturing investments. A possible explanation for these results is that mining investments require fairly extensive technical negotiations early on pertaining to access to markets and to marketing procedures for raw materials in the home country, while facilitating the inputs associated with manufacturing investments may only require a verbal diplomatic effort. Clearly, these differences in the initial foreign policy behavior associated with mining and manufacturing investments should serve as the focus of future research.

The second variation from the expected results pertains to the cooperation and conflict found after nine years. The relationships found were not limited just to poor countries with a high concentration of investments, but applied to all countries. After approximately a decade, a high stock of foreign investment in manufacturing appears to create an interest in autonomy that is felt in all countries, regardless of their level of development and degree of dependence. This concern, however, appears to be tempered by the desire, as mentioned above, to maintain the ongoing flow of inputs needed to complement the foreign manufacturing presence.

A comparison of the manufacturing and mining results shows that the R^2 values associated with the manufacturing findings are not as high as for mining.

Table 2.3

Six-Year Time-Lag Results for Cooperation and Conflict with the Largest Foreign National Source of Mining Investments

Dependent Variable	TotInvMin	LoDevel x HiConcen x TotInvMin	HiDevel x HiConcen x TotInvMin	Pop	Debt	R^2
Security	-.15			-.05	-.03	-.06
Cooperation		.03		.00	-.03	-.09
			-.18	-.04	-.02	-.06
Economic and	.08			-.02	-.37*	.06
Technical		-.50***		-.03	-.36*	.33
Cooperation			.09	-.02	-.38*	.06
Verbal	-.12			-.04	.29	.02
Cooperation		.65***		-.01	.27	.47
			-.19	-.04	.30	.04
Verbal	.15			-.08	-.12	-.04
Conflict		-.26		-.12	-.11	.01
			.28	-.06	-.13	.01
Economic	-.11			.16	.37*	.06
and Technical		-.24		.19	.38*	.11
Conflict			-.06	.18	.38*	.05

Note: 38 is the sample size.
*p<.05
***p<.001

At a statistical level, this indicates that variables not considered in the analysis are affecting the foreign policy behavior displayed toward the largest foreign source of manufacturing investments. At a more theoretical level, this implies that when foreign investments are in mining, the preoccupation with foreign investment, and hence the effect on foreign policy, is greater than it is when the investments are in the manufacturing sector. The probable reason for this has been discussed previously—host state officials are more suspicious of mining investments, questioning their contribution to local development and expecting threats to local autonomy. Hence, there is a feeling of a need for action, and the effect of foreign policy behavior is stronger. The more benign appearance of manufacturing investments, which seem to aid local development more, pro-duces less of a sense of urgency, and other variables are considered when formulating foreign policy. Future research should investigate thoroughly the nature of these variables and their possible relationships to foreign investment.

The results for the control variables show that a large population is associated with more security cooperation early on, leads to more economic and technical cooperation with the mining investor's home country after three years, and is associated with more economic and technical conflict over the longer run. Larger countries appear to move from a willingness to cooperate toward attempts to assert independence of action and to reduce the role of foreigners in their societies as time passes. The findings for external debt display a similar pattern, with

Table 2.4

Nine-Year Time-Lag Results for Cooperation and Conflict with the Largest Foreign National Source of Mining Investments

Dependent Variable	TotInvMin	LoDevel x HiConcen x TotInvMin	HiDevel x HiConcen x TotInvMin	Pop	Debt	R^2
Security Cooperation	-.06			.25	.31	.03
		-.22		.34	.34	.08
			-.05	.25	.31	.03
Economic and Technical Cooperation	-.17			-.32	-.04	.00
		-.13		-.23	-.03	-.02
			.00	-.27	-.06	-.03
Verbal Cooperation	.13			-.05	.03	-.08
		.22		-.16	.00	-.05
			-.07	-.11	.06	-.09
Verbal Conflict	.16			.19	-.18	-.02
		-.31		.24	-.11	.05
			.20	.20	-.19	-.01
Economic and Technical Conflict	.00			.52**	-.04	.21
		.45**		.38*	-.13	.41
			.00	.52**	-.04	.21

Note: 31 is the sample size.
*p<.05
**p<.01

higher debt being associated with more economic and technical cooperation early on and less such cooperation and more economic and technical conflict over time. One anomaly in the debt results is the positive association for security cooperation with the manufacturing investor's home country after nine years. While it is beyond the scope of the present effort to address systematically the reasons for this result, future research should pursue this matter.

CONCLUSIONS

The first conclusion suggested by the analysis in this chapter is that foreign investments lead to interdependence between the home and host states and to scapegoating. In general, the effects of this interdependence are centered in poor countries with higher total stocks from a single foreign national source and shift over time as the host country seeks to balance its need for economic well-being and its desire for autonomy. The results obtained in this chapter imply the need for some slight refinements regarding the effects of interdependence. For one thing, instead of the initial warm reception that was hypothesized, the findings indicate that the ambivalence toward mining investments is found early on. Host officials seem inclined only toward extending such cooperation as is necessary for obtaining benefits, but appear to distrust the foreign presence from the start. At first, the host state must engage in economic and technical cooperation to set

Table 2.5
Synchronic Results for Cooperation and Conflict with the Largest Foreign National Source of Manufacturing Investments

Dependent Variable	TotInvMan	LoDevel x HiConcen x TotInvMan	HiDevel x HiConcen x TotInvMan	Pop	Debt	R^2
Security	.00			.30*	.11	.06
Cooperation		.02		.31*	.11	.06
			.23	.35**	.14	.11
Economic and	-.20			-.09	.26*	.07
Technical		-.18		-.05	.30*	.06
Cooperation			.21	.01	.31*	.07
Verbal	-.03			.05	-.06	-.05
Cooperation		-.02		.06	-.06	-.05
			.00	.06	-.06	-.05
Verbal	.04			-.07	-.23	.01
Conflict		.13		-.06	-.24	.03
			-.18	-.11	-.25	.04
Economic and	.24			.07	-.06	.00
Technical		.06		.00	-.08	-.05
Conflict			-.10	-.02	-.09	-.04

Note: 58 is the sample size.
*$p<.05$
**$p<.01$

up the appropriate marketing procedures, but other forms of cooperation are not extended. Over time, the expansion of the role of foreigners in the host society is limited (and autonomy is protected) by cutting back on technical cooperation, but at the same time there is an effort to continue receiving benefits through the extension of diplomatic cooperation. Finally, the concern with autonomy and the perception that foreigners are contributing little to local development merge, and the foreign role is cut back. It appears to take little more than a decade for this process to run its course.

In the manufacturing sector, the required refinement has to do with the degree to which the concern with autonomy is general over time among all states and is not centered just among those that are poorest and most dependent. It was expected that their greater resource availability would make states at higher levels of development less prone to worry about autonomy. The results imply, however, that with the passage of time the desire to ensure one's freedom of action is found more universally among countries with higher stocks of investments in manufacturing. Apparently, suspicions surrounding a large foreign presence are ubiquitous and extend to all sectors, even those, such as manufacturing, where there is a belief that the foreign presence contributes to local economic well-being.

A second conclusion of this chapter is that foreign investments do not seem to have the sort of Trojan Horse effects that are discussed in the literature.

Table 2.6

Three-Year Time-Lag Results for Cooperation and Conflict with the Largest Foreign National Source of Manufacturing Investments

Dependent Variable	TotInvMan	LoDevel x HiConcen x TotInvMan	HiDevel x HiConcen x TotInvMan	Pop	Debt	R^2
Security	-.02			.14	.17	.00
Cooperation		-.03		.14	.17	.00
			.00	.15	.17	.00
Economic and	-.19			.07	.04	.00
Technical		-.10		.12	.06	-.02
Cooperation			.03	.13	.08	-.03
Verbal	.32*			.00	-.10	.08
‚Cooperation		.28*		-.08	-.13	.06
			.00	-.10	-.17	-.01
Verbal	-.18			-.07	.05	-.02
Conflict		-.24		-.05	.06	.01
			-.13	-.05	.08	-.03
Economic and	-.01			.03	-.07	-.05
Technical		-.01		.04	-.07	-.05
Conflict			.12	.06	-.05	-.03

Note: 58 is the sample size.

*p<.05

Neither the mining nor the manufacturing results were consistent with the expectations of this conception. Three contingencies present themselves. The first is that multinational corporations have Trojan Horse effects only under certain international conditions. A. G. Frank (1969:9–10) and Bodenheimer (1971:160) argue that periods of severe depression and/or war among dominant industrial states have a significant effect upon the degree of domination experienced by underdeveloped countries. Gobalet and Diamond (1979:438–39) and Rubinson (1977:22–23) concur, and Rothgeb's (1986a) research supports the contention that the role of foreign investment in the Third World changes when recessions occur in developed countries. It is possible that the comparative analysis of time periods in which dominant states experience different levels of internecine conflict and/or economic depression would provide support for the Trojan Horse model.

A second possibility is that the identity of the home state has an effect on the role played by foreign investors. Magdoff (1969) regards the use of foreign investments as an instrument of control as most characteristic of the United States. Chase-Dunn (1978) and Chase-Dunn and Rubinson (1979) generalize this point, maintaining that when one industrialized state eclipses all others in strength, it uses its economic ties to underdeveloped countries to exert domination. Recent empirical research indicates that the effects of foreign investments do indeed change according to the home country of origin (Rothgeb, 1986a).

Table 2.7
Six-Year Time-Lag Results for Cooperation and Conflict with the Largest Foreign National Source of Manufacturing Investments

Dependent Variable	TotInvMan	LoDevel x HiConcen x TotInvMan	HiDevel x HiConcen x TotInvMan	Pop	Debt	R²
Security	.04			.12	-.07	-.03
Cooperation		.07		.11	-.08	-.03
			-.19	.06	-.12	.00
Economic and	-.36**			.10	-.03	.11
Technical		-.44***		.16	.02	.18
Cooperation			.18	.22	.02	.01
Verbal	.37**			-.24	-.05	.19
Cooperation		.42***		-.30*	-.10	.22
			-.19	-.37**	-.09	.08
Verbal	-.22			.07	-.07	.02
Conflict		-.18		.10	-.05	.00
			.05	.13	-.06	-.03
Economic and	.07			.28*	.29*	.07
Technical		.11		.27*	.28*	.07
Conflict			.03	.28*	.30*	.06

Note: 59 is the sample size.
*p<.05
**p<.01
***p<.001

Further research should investigate the patterns of relationships found when the effects of investments from differing home states are compared.

The third contingency is that if an international structure of control does exist, then either multinational corporations are not its central agents or control is vested in other areas of political, social, and economic activity, and foreign policy behavior is left unaffected. The next chapter turns to the investigation of the final possibility, as attention centers on the effects of foreign investment on domestic political and social behavior in underdeveloped host countries.

NOTES

1. Hermann's (1978:34) definition of foreign policy behavior is used. According to Hermann, foreign policy behavior is

the discrete purposeful action that results from the political level decision of an individual or group of individuals. Political level decision makers are those whose authority is required to commit or withhold those resources of a nation that are available to those who govern. Thus, a [foreign policy] behavior is viewed as the observable artifact of a political level decision. It is not the decision, but a product of the decision.

2. Stocks of foreign investment are defined as the total value of the holdings of foreign investors in the host state. Flows are the value of new capital that is introduced into a country during a specific period of time.

Table 2.8

Nine-Year Time-Lag Results for Cooperation and Conflict with the Largest Foreign National Source of Manufacturing Investments

Dependent Variable	TotInvMan	LoDevel x HiConcen x TotInvMan	HiDevel x HiConcen x TotInvMan	Pop	Debt	R^2
Security	-.07			.13	.57***	.28
Cooperation		-.21		.13	.63***	.32
			.05	.16	.57***	.28
Economic and	-.30*			-.27	.18	.08
Technical		-.07		-.18	.19	.00
Cooperation			-.05	-.18	.16	.00
Verbal	.46**			.07	-.13	.15
Cooperation		.30		-.05	-.19	.04
			-.03	-.09	-.10	-.05
Verbal	-.16			.18	-.23	.09
Conflict		-.23		.21	-.17	.11
			.16	.28	-.22	.09
Economic and	.00			.31*	-.15	.07
Technical		-.03		.30*	-.14	.07
Conflict			-.02	.30*	-.15	.07

Note: 48 is the sample size.
*p<.05
**p<.01
***p<.001

3. For the most part, the authors who discuss foreign investments as a means for controlling underdeveloped countries are from what McGowan and Smith (1978:184) refer to as the Marxist and dependency schools of thought. In addition to McGowan and Smith, Cohen (1973:99–227) provides a careful analysis of these bodies of literature, and Caporaso (1978a; 1978b; 1980) discusses dependency theory excellently.

4. Scholars who have investigated scapegoating as a social phenomenon note that it is an act of hostility that is a product of frustration and that it often is directed at foreigners because hostility can be "expressed against these groups without restraint or expectation of retaliation" (Adorno et al., 1969:485). Bergeson (1977:220–33) reports that directing hostility toward outsiders often is perceived as a means for cementing a society together. Bonazzi (1983) found that scapegoating involves very symbolic behavior designed to persuade an audience and requires that the target of hostility be highly visible to those one wishes to impress, and Eagle and Newton's (1981) research indicates that those selected as scapegoats usually have previously antagonized in some way those who turn on them.

5. As Moran (1974) skillfully illustrates, while the host government may perceive that a lack of vulnerability exists because officials may feel that local managers and workers can operate mines effectively, a reliance upon market structures in the home country may continue. Moran notes that this latter form of vulnerability tends to be downplayed and has much less effect on host government decision making than considerations relating to the operation of mining enterprises.

6. The author is aware of the various problems Mahler (1980:5–13) mentions in his

excellent discussion of the uses of cross-national designs but agrees that such research provides valuable insight into the relationships investigated. It should be noted that the actual sample size of each statistical test is less than 84 due to missing data for some countries in the data set. The SPSSX (1983) package was used to conduct the analysis. A Select If command was employed to select only cases for which there were complete data. This procedure is used in the analysis in each chapter of this book. The problem of missing data tends to affect states from all geographic regions of the Third World and therefore should not introduce undue bias into the results. Lists of the specific countries that are included in each statistical test are available from the author upon request.

7. Acts of military conflict were not included because they occurred very infrequently. For the time periods examined, six states or fewer engaged in such behavior.

8. COPDAB was selected in preference to other events data sets for four reasons: (1) its sample of states had the greatest overlap with the 84 examined herein, (2) it is based upon multiple news sources (70 in all), (3) the time periods covered were well suited to the present needs, and (4) the COPDAB international scale was well suited for the operationalizations needed herein. Excellent discussions of the several events data sets are available from Burgess and Lawton (1975) and Kegley (1975).

9. External public debt is defined as including both direct governmental borrowing payable in foreign currency and maturing in more than one year from financial institutions located beyond the government's sovereign jurisdiction and government guarantees of such borrowing by quasi-governmental and nongovernmental agencies (World Bank, 1980:9; Frieden, 1981:409). Frieden (1981:407) and Lipson (1981:603–4) note that external borrowing by underdeveloped countries increased dramatically during the time periods examined herein, sharply increasing the resource pool these states could draw upon.

10. The sources used to obtain the data reported monetary values in United States dollars; thus, there was no need to convert local currency to dollars. When monetary values were not reported in constant 1970 dollars, the deflator for gross domestic product provided by the World Bank (1976, 1980, 1983) was used.

11. Nie et al. (1975:381–83) and Lewis-Beck (1980:54–56) recommend the use of dummy variables for constructing interaction terms. Using this technique allows the researcher to assess the nature of the relationship between the independent and dependent variables for states that possess particular characteristics (in this case, a high concentration of investments from one foreign national source and either a high or a low level of development). One is able to do this because the dummy variables have values of zero for states that do not possess the characteristics of interest, thereby reducing the value of the interaction term for such states to zero. As a result, the regression slope for the interaction term reflects the association between the independent and dependent variables for states that have the characteristics of interest, making it possible to determine whether these states display the hypothesized relationship. Within the present context, an attempt was made to ensure that the results obtained for the interaction term were not a product of the manner in which the dummy variable was constructed. This was done by using different cutoff points when creating the dummy variable representing a high concentration of foreign investments from the largest foreign national source. In addition to using .70 as the cutoff point, the analysis was replicated using the median (.61 for mining and .65 for manufacturing) and .80. The same procedure was followed in each of the other chapters in this book. In each case, the results were the same as those reported.

12. The reader should realize that this does not imply that all of the relationships

followed linear patterns. Instead, it means that no clear nonlinear patterns that would warrant data transformations were evident.

13. Lewis-Beck (1980:54–56) notes that the use of fully saturated models (see Nie et al., 1975:382) in regression analysis with interaction terms often results in problems with multicollinearity. The solution suggested is the use of separate regression equations that examine the main effects and interaction terms individually (see Lewis-Beck, 1980:59). This solution has one side effect, however, for it vastly increases the size of the tables required for reporting the results. In order to conserve space, the practice followed herein is to include only the findings for the variables that are of immediate theoretical relevance. These include the main effects of stocks of investment in mining and manufacturing and the effects of the interaction terms. The findings for the dummy variables for high concentration and for high and low development are omitted from the tables but are available from the author upon request.

14. One also should note that sectoral breakdowns for the total stock of foreign investment only are available for 1967. The same is true for data pertaining to the breakdown of total stock according to foreign national source. Data for more recent years are for total stock, with no indication of sector or foreign national source. The dearth of data for sectoral location or for foreign national source was not considered a serious flaw in the present context because the basic time-lagged research design was workable with the data available.

15. Each of the tables in this and subsequent chapters report beta weights. The R^2 values are adjusted for the sample size and for the number of independent variables in the equation. The level of significance of the beta weights is indicated as follows: *$p<.05$, **$p<.01$, ***$p<.001$, and ****$p<.0001$.

3

Liberalizer or Repressor: Foreign Investment and Domestic Politics

Foreign investments are often described as having a far-reaching impact upon the domestic political environment found in underdeveloped host states. As is the case with virtually everything that is associated with multinational corporate activities in the Third World, the precise nature of these effects is regarded by most authors as complex and is the subject of a wide-ranging debate. The crux of the dispute centers around how theorists view the interplay between the vast capabilities and influence that the corporation is presumed to have and the assumption made by many scholars that the political and social processes in host countries profoundly affect the ability of the corporation to do business and to secure a profit.

As was discussed in the introduction, multinational corporations have vast resource bases and are regarded as possessing great influence in poor countries. At the same time, one finds general agreement both among analysts who are very critical of foreign investments and among those who are more supportive that certain domestic environments are perceived by corporations as more conducive to doing business than others. Key areas of disagreement emerge regarding the type of political atmosphere preferred by multinational firms and whether the corporation uses its capabilities and influence to mold the domestic environment to suit its tastes.

In general, two basic views are found in the literature regarding the type of environment the corporation prefers. The first centers around the supposition that the corporation encourages repressive and nonreformist social policies to ensure that it obtains the maximum return in profits from its operations. The second regards foreign investors as having a liberalizing effect, providing exposure to foreign conceptions of how to manage a society and placing the resources necessary to implement reforms at the disposal of the host state.

Two conceptions also are found as to whether the corporation actively uses its influence to shape the domestic environment. One is built around a set of views that are similar to the Trojan Horse framework, with the corporation and the local government being regarded as cooperating as allies. Some theorists see the foreign firm as the preponderant partner in this alliance, and others regard the firm as unable to dominate the host government but as working closely with the government, establishing a symbiotic relationship wherein the corporation provides resources to strengthen the government and the state uses its power to suppress social conditions that the corporation finds unacceptable. A second conception regards corporate impacts on host society political and social conditions as the produce of an indirect and informal set of influences. Many analysts see these influences as malevolent, encouraging an ever-widening gulf between the elite and the masses that ends in less social reform and more repression. Other analysts, expressing views similar to those found in the non–Foreign Entity framework, believe these influences create a more liberal climate in the host society.

Previous cross-national research regarding the social effects of foreign investment has generally focused on social distribution and inequality instead of upon politics and governmental policy. Bornschier, et al. (1978:653–70) and Bornschier and Chase-Dunn (1985:69–71, 117–30) provide excellent summaries of these studies; hence, there is no need to repeat that exercise here. Among the work to date, only two studies have investigated the effects of the multinational corporation upon the strength of the host government. Rubinson (1977:20) found no relationship between the income foreign investors earn from their holdings and governmental strength, and Mahler (1981:288) found a positive relationship between stocks of investment in mining and the direct taxes collected by the government. In neither of these studies, however, was an attempt made to determine the time frame within which these effects occurred through the use of time-lagged analysis, nor was there an effort to determine how the effect, or lack of an effect, on governmental strength affected the social policies pursued by the government.

The purpose of this chapter is to investigate the impact of foreign investments upon the domestic political and social behavior found in Third World states. The discussion shall focus on several key variables: (1) the degree to which the government plays a dominant role in regulating and managing society, (2) the extent to which the government pursues policies designed to introduce social reforms to improve the lost of the common citizen, (3) the government's use of repression to squash domestic opposition, and (4) the level of domestic political conflict found in the host society. The varying conceptions outlined above regarding how foreign investments affect local political and social conditions are discussed very briefly. Following this, systematic empirical techniques are used to analyze the interrelationships between foreign investment and the above variables.

FOREIGN INVESTMENT AND
HOST COUNTRY POLITICS

Asymmetrical Alliance

A convenient starting point for discussing foreign investment and host country politics is the alliance between the local elite and the foreign corporation. Two views of this alliance are found in the literature. The first sees the alliance as asymmetrical because of the tremendous resources available to the corporation and the great need the local elite has for foreign support in handling its relations with its own people. The second regards the corporation and the host government as working together as near equals.

The asymmetrical alliance is based on a community of interests between the elite and the multinational firm. The common interest of both is social stability. The elite favors stability because the maintenance of the status quo guarantees that it can retain its dominant social position. The corporation is interested in stability because it fears that social upheaval might deprive it of its property and of the ability to do business. Thus, the two associate closely with one another, and "what results is a political and social coalition of wealthy compradors, powerful monopolists, and large landowners dedicated to the defense of the existing feudal-mercantile order" (Baran, 1957:195).

While this coalition may be mutually convenient, it is hardly based upon shared amity, and its advantages are not distributed evenly. Rubinson (1976:643–44; 1977:8–9) notes that the corporation has a strong interest in keeping the host government weak and in limiting its ability to regulate society. There are several reasons for doing this. One is that the corporation may not trust its local allies, believing that forces such as nationalism and a desire to display independence may at some point tempt the local elite to act against corporate interests. A weak government reduces the need for trust, for an impotent host government is in no position to take action against the firm and thus poses a much smaller potential threat (Baran, 1957:197).

A second reason the corporation desires a weak local governmental ally is that such a government is less able to regulate foreign investors by monitoring their operations and taxing their profits (Chase-Dunn and Rubinson, 1977:468). A third is that feeble governments are almost completely at the mercy of the corporation and are highly dependent on the firm for support, rendering them "largely incapable of independent action or initiative" (Magdoff and Sweezy, 1971:111). In such a situation, foreign investors may have a free hand to exploit the host society as they wish without any fear of meaningful interference from the captive local government.

Therefore, multinational corporations are depicted as working to keep host governments weak in order to prevent "the threat of truly independent regimes" (Bodenheimer, 1971:174). This goal is accomplished through the use of the superior resource base that the corporation has in comparison with the host government and because of the local elite's greater intensity of involvement in the relationship. As noted in earlier chapters, many multinational corporations have far greater available pools of resource than do underdeveloped hosts, especially when the host society is very poor. At the same time, the host government's intensity of involvement in its association with the corporation may be greater because it may perceive itself as needing the corporation in order to retain its social position. Thus, the local elite may regard the cost of losing the support of the corporation as very high, for the price envisioned may be social revolution and a complete loss of status (Magdoff and Sweezy, 1971:111). As was discussed previously, these types of perceptions should be most prevalent when the host society is highly dependent, that is, when the stock of foreign investment is very high and is overwhelmingly from a single foreign national source.

Richardson (1978:7–8) observes that many authors believe that the collaboration between the foreigners and the local elite have severe detrimental effects upon the host society as a whole. Three basic political and social consequences are discussed as resulting from an asymmetrical alliance of this sort. The first is that since its position of social dominance is guaranteed by the support of its multinational ally, the local elite has little incentive to institute social reforms to improve the condition of the masses. Such reforms are seen by scholars with this point of view as being a product of an interplay between the masses and an elite that must depend upon the people for support. The elite's association with foreign firms means that the dependent regime need not concern itself with the masses. Hence, reforms are ignored (Brundenius, 1972:200; Magdoff, 1976:216–17; Rubinson, 1977:8–9).

The second consequence is a product of the same forces that produce the first. Because it does not rely on the people for support, the dependent regime does not need to open up the political process to allow greater participation for nonelite segments of society. According to Magdoff and Sweezy (1971:112), "peasants and workers are largely excluded from the political arena." In addition, its overly close relationship with foreigners leaves the regime "void of any legitimacy as a ruling class" (Pinelo, 1973:x). The result of the combined effects of these two factors and of the lack of any social reform is a higher level of political conflict in the host society as the masses express their dissatisfaction.

The third consequence of the alliance is that the host government is forced to rely upon repression to hold on to power. Repression is necessary in part because the regime lacks legitimacy. As Baran (1957:195) states, the "regime has no real political basis in city or village, lives in continual fear of the starving and restive popular masses, and relies for its stability on Praetorian guards of relatively well kept mercenaries." Repression also is used as a response to political protest. Bodenheimer (1971:178) argues that "dependent or comprador governments, subservient to foreign interests, are forced to employ overt repression . . . against popular movements."

Thus, the asymmetrical alliance is regarded as resulting in a docile and weaker host government that has a limited ability to regulate society, that does not introduce social reform, that confronts greater levels of political conflict (because it refuses to allow political participation for the masses, it lacks legitimacy, and it holds back on social reforms), and that acts repressively to control society. These regimes are seen as existing only because they are supported by foreign interests:

That they have been able to stay in business—for business is, indeed, their sole concern . . . is due mainly if not exclusively to the aid and support that was given to them "freely" by Western capital. . . . [T]he maintenance of these regimes and the operations of foreign enterprise in the underdeveloped countries have become mutually interdependent. . . . It is the preservation of these subservient governments, stifling economic and social development and suppressing all popular movements for social and national liberation, that makes possible . . . the continued foreign exploitation (Baran, 1957:196).

Symmetrical Alliance

A very different state of affairs is pictured by those who see the alliance between foreign investors and the host government as symmetrical, constituting a union of near equals. Such an association may only exist when the host government is capable of matching the resources of the multinational corporation and possesses assets that the corporation values highly, thus reducing the asymmetry in the intensity of involvement that the corporation and host government have in their relationship with one another. Both requirements are met when the host society is at a high level of development. Rubinson (1977:20–21) points out that the level of development of the host country has a profound effect upon host/firm relations. As was discussed in the preceding chapter, a higher level of development enables the host state to tap more of its resources and use them more efficiently, thereby effectively enlarging its resource base. At the same time, a wealthier society has both a desirable market and a usable pool of labor, both of which are assets that the corporation may be expected to covet. In addition, Apter (1976:30) notes that in societies at higher levels of development the state bureaucracy is sufficiently strong that it "provides political controls, mobilizes basic resources, establishes technical and fiscal networks, and has the power to generate an institutional infrastructure favorable to the multinationals."

Thus, while the poorest members of the Third World find themselves confronted with an asymmetrical situation because they lack the ability to tap resources, the markets, the skilled labor, and the more sophisticated bureaucratic structure found in wealthier countries, the positions of wealthier states are more advantageous. In more developed societies, the hypothesized alliance between foreign firms and the host elite is based on common advantage. As Fagen (1978:292–95), Cardoso and Faletto (1979:163–64), and Sunkel (1979:223) discuss, the local government provides the corporation with access to its markets in exchange for assistance in promoting the accumulation of resources to benefit the elite and cement its hold on power.

Evans (1979) provides an excellent description of the relative advantages accruing to the host government and the firm within the context of the symmetrical alliance. The primary advantage for the host government is the corporate desire to do business and to locate production facilities within the wealthier Third World society. This desire makes the firm reliant upon the host government not only for access to markets, but also for the maintenance of the host economy and for the protection of its assets. The foreign investor cooperates with the government in order to ensure that the proper economic climate is sustained for doing business and to guarantee the sort of social order needed to safeguard its investments. In effect, the firm's local subsidiary becomes a hostage of the host government, which is strong enough to mold local conditions either to favor the subsidiary or to harm it. For its part, the host government depends upon the foreign firm for the entrepreneurial talent, the capital, and especially the technology needed to promote development in the host society and to increase the resources at the disposal of the government so that it may remain in office. On balance, the corporation trades its technological competence to the state for the type of political environment that it regards as favorable for business. As Evans (1979:203) says, "The best cards on the side of the locals are political. The multinational's best cards are technological."

According to Evans (1979:9–11), local entrepreneurs join the symmetrical alliance between foreign investors and the host government as a third partner. These members of the local elite contribute an understanding of the local market and how to exploit it and provide a commercial network of suppliers and distributors that aids foreign investors in doing business and facilitates governmental control over vital parts of society (Evans, 1979:136).

With the combined strength of these three partners, the alliance is able to pursue a strategy designed to ensure progress in the host society. In fact, progress becomes the overriding objective of the coalition and is especially foremost in the minds of the governmental members of the alliance, who tend to perceive the promotion of development as the primary duty of the government and as a means for guaranteeing their incumbency. Other members of the alliance benefit from progress as well, for it means better markets and more profits both for foreign and local capital (Evans, 1979:48–49).

Within the context of pursuing this goal, speed and efficiency become paramount concerns, for there is a desire to move ahead as rapidly as possible. The result is a hard attitude both toward social reform and toward extending political participation and a share in social decision making to those who are not in the coalition. Opening the political process and instituting reforms both require the allocation of resources. Such an expenditure would detract from the vast resources required for quick development. Moreover, wider political participation may be seen as inefficient, for it involves the use of valuable resources for the purpose of allowing nonspecialists to take part in the making of key social and economic decisions. Hence, the alliance sets itself against both social reform and nonelite political participation. The people are expected to contribute to the progress of society as a whole by being acquiescent and by allowing the members of the coalition a freer hand in managing society (Fagen, 1978:292–95; Evans, 1979:29–31; Leonard, 1980:460–61).

The results of these attitudes are higher levels of political protest and repression. The refusal to implement reforms to allow the benefits of development to reach the people as a whole and the closing of the political system to those who are not in the alliance produce political conflict. The response to such protest is repression, for it is seen by the elite as an attempt to disrupt the pursuit of policies that are designed to bring progress to society as a whole (Evans, 1979:49).

Political conflict also may come from two other sources. The first is from some members of the local entrepreneurial class who are concerned that they are being excluded from participating in the economic development of society. The inclusion of foreign manufacturing firms as key elements in the alliance means that "the core of private manufacturing is increasingly foreign," confronting many local businessmen with an unpalatable situation (Evans, 1979:152). Political protest designed to encourage the government to take action to alleviate this problem is a product of this situation (Barnet and Muller, 1974:190). Another source of political conflict centers around foreign investments in the mining sector. Evans (1979:201–2) points out that only manufacturing enterprises are included in the alliance between foreigners and the local elite, for these types of firms are perceived as having valuable contributions to make to the development of the host society. Investments in mining, however, are seen as making little contribution to development and are regarded as exploitative. Hence, foreign mining enterprises are discussed as being the source of considerable political conflict in the host country.

To summarize, theorists who discuss the symmetrical alliance see it as occurring between foreign manufacturing firms and host governmental officials and private entrepreneurs in underdeveloped countries at higher levels of development. Such an alliance produces a stronger host government capable of regulating society extensively and encourages the pursuit of policies that are designed to promote quick development and that are inimical to social reform and wider political participation. This creates greater political conflict and repression.

Malevolent Influence

A third set of views pertaining to the political and social effects of foreign investments is held by scholars who regard the multinational corporation as exerting influence much as would a powerful and somewhat malevolent pressure group. Analysts adopting this position do not posit an alliance between the corporation and the host elite, but do see the foreign presence as having many effects that are similar to those discussed by alliance theorists. Two strands of thought are found within this framework. One focuses upon the effects of foreign investment on the role the host government plays in society, while the other is devoted more to the consequences of a large foreign presence for the government's political and social policies.

The first strand of thought is based on the premise that governments in underdeveloped countries do not enjoy a situation in which their societies are dominated by foreigners. One policy response that is designed to prevent a large foreign investment presence from leading to foreign domination is the government expanding greatly the role it plays in society, thereby allowing the government to counterbalance the role played by foreigners (Cardoso and Faletto, 1979:165; Duvall and Freeman, 1981:113). Host governments are especially oriented toward counterbalancing when the size of the foreign presence is large in the most modern parts of the host economy, such as in the manufacturing sector (Rothgeb, 1986b:140). Duvall and Freeman (1983:573) argue that counterbalancing the foreign presence requires a very large pool of resources and that in underdeveloped states only the government has access to such resources, forcing it to play the part of a state entrepreneur. The resource requirement also restricts the use of such a strategy to governments that rule wealthier Third World countries.

Resorting to a counterbalancing strategy may be viewed by the government not only as a means to keep host country dependence to a tolerable level, but also as contributing to two other important goals. One is that it promotes growth and development. The second is that it helps keep the government's political leadership in good standing with three important political groupings within society: (1) international capital, (2) the national bourgeoisie, and (3) the technobureaucratic elite (Duvall and Freeman, 1981:113). International capital benefits because a larger government role expands the economy and creates the potential for more business and profits. The national bourgeoisie gains to the extent that foreigners are not allowed to dominate completely the local scene. The technobureaucratic elite that is charged with managing the government's participation in society profits because its position as a key element in society is enhanced as that participation increases.

Duvall and Freeman (1983:579–81) regard the need to maintain the support of these three groups as being of paramount importance to the government. It is in considering this point that a significant difference emerges between symmetrical alliance theorists and those adhering to the present views. Alliance theorists see foreign investors as a part of a coalition that manages society and regard multinational corporations as contributing to the upkeep on that coalition in order to assure its dominance. Malevolence theorists, however, do not see an alliance; instead they see a situation in which a large foreign investment presence creates the need for a vastly expanded governmental role, but does not necessarily pay upkeep of any sort. In fact, Duvall and Freeman (1983:579) discuss the government as being forced to expand its activities in response to multinational corporate behavior. When foreign firms fail to increase their investments at the proper rate, then the overall pool of resources for promoting growth and development falls, and the government must make up the difference by raising its contribution and playing a larger role in society or else risk losing the support of some key elements in society that back the government only so long as the requisite level of growth in resource availability is maintained.

The social consequences of the above pattern are described as a government that focuses too much upon counterbalancing and therefore becomes divorced from the people as a whole. The result is a failure to ensure that the benefits of development reach the masses through the promotion of reforms, a failure which leads to political conflict and repression (Cardoso and Faletto, 1979:166–70; Duvall and Freeman, 1981:109).

Another conception of how the multinational corporation exerts a malevolent influence focuses on the effects of a large foreign presence on the local class structure. As Jackson et al. (1978:633) state, the "increasing cultural dependence of the regime on the capitalist center will weaken the traditional class base of the state." Foreign investors are seen as introducing foreign values and culture that are accepted by the local elite as superior to indigenous customs (Cardoso and Faletto, 1979:xvi; Sunkel, 1979:223; Mahler, 1981:272). Chief among these values are an attachment to the goal of progress and a consumer orientation (Barnet and Muller, 1974:172–78; Mahler, 1981:272).

Acceptance of these foreign values and pursuit of development that is designed to allow for greater consumption by the elite create an ever wider gulf between the rulers and the ruled (Leonard, 1980:464; Mahler, 1981:272). The result is an increasing marginalization of the masses, as reforms are not employed to extend the ability to consume to the people (Jackson et al., 1978:631; Bornschier and Ballmer-Cao, 1979:488). This leads to what Jackson et al. (1978:631) label *latent conflict*, which refers to the building up of frustration and resentment among the people. Latent conflict manifests itself over time in higher levels of political conflict, to which, as Jackson et al. (1978:634) assume, an instinctive governmental response is repression.

To summarize, foreign investments are seen as having a malevolent influence in two ways. The first is by forcing the host government to expand its role in managing society to counterbalance the foreign presence, which soaks up resources to such an extent that social reforms are impossible, leading to political conflict and repression. The second does not see the multinational presence as operating by way of an effect on the government's role in society, but instead posits an effect on the local class structure that stifles reform and produces greater political conflict and more repression.

Liberalizing Influence

The collection of views regarded as falling under the liberalizing rubric are built around the same basic type of assumption that was the foundation of the non–Foreign Entity conception discussed in the preceding chapter. This is that foreign investors seek to fit unobtrusively into the social and political environment found in Third World states and do not use their capabilities to mold the domestic arena. Vernon (1976:47–48) argues that the internationally oriented strategies of multinational corporations dictate that they forego too close a political involvement in any particular host state lest it restrict their ability to attain key corporate objectives. Indeed, their foreign origins are seen as surrounding the firm with a sufficient degree of suspicion that it is forced to avoid becoming too much involved in local politics because such participation may hamper its ability to do business (I. Frank, 1980:41). Of course, foreign firms are inevitably drawn into local political and social issues, but most authors from this school of thought regard such activities as minimal.

Liberal theorists generally repudiate the notion that any sort of alliance exists between foreign investors and the local elite. As Moran (1974:247) says:

[T]he Chilean experience suggests that foreign investors in prominent natural-resource industries in developing countries have few permanent domestic allies. In the course of history their lives become increasingly solitary, poor, nasty, brutish, and short.

Sklar (1975:176) makes a similar point regarding mining investments in Zambia. The rejection of the possibility of an alliance extends to the manufacturing sector, too. I. Frank (1980:41) argues that foreign manufacturing firms operate in the most highly prized sector of the host economy. They are the subject of close scrutiny and are jealously monitored by a local government that perceives the activity of these firms as a potential threat to the government's position as the leading actor on the local scene. Diaz-Alejandro (1970:331), Keohane and Ooms (1972:110), and Richardson (1978:41–42) agree. In fact, Vernon (1971:197) and Moran (1978:93–94) see governmental technobureaucrats and members of the local business community, the very domestic groups that are posited as forming parts of the symmetrical triple alliance mentioned above, as being unlikely allies because of their deep hostility toward foreign firms.

It is within this context that foreign investments are discussed as affecting local political and social processes and structures. An important impact on the local scene is regarded as resulting from the increase in resources that comes from corporate activities. Reuber (1973:218) states that in countries with a large foreign presence, the reinvestments of corporate profits and the introduction of new capital from abroad constitutes a substantial addition to the society's overall resource availability and will create over time an ability for the government to increase its strength and its ability to regulate society. Vernon (1976:51–52) and I. Frank (1980:30) see a similar effect, maintaining that foreign investment stimulates the sort of economic activity that leads over time to an expanding pool of resources that may be used by the government.

Liberal theorists do not deny that foreign influences encourage consumption by the elite, but they argue that the result is not a grossly distorted class structure and a refusal to institute social reform (Vernon, 1971:181–85; 1977:53). Instead, they see a trickle-down effect wherein corporate activities and increases in investments lead to an expansion of resources that results over time in new social programs to help the masses (Reuber, 1973:37, 218; I. Frank, 1980:31). Foreign investment also is regarded as providing technology that allows for the more efficient use of local resources, creating a greater ability to promote reform over time (Gilpin, 1975:58).

As far as political conflict is concerned, foreign investment is seen as disrupting the host society, but not for the reasons discussed above, for multinational firms are not regarded as having a dampening effect on political participation, legitimacy, and social reform. Increases in political conflict are treated as a product of more direct effects: (1) the introduction of new values that undermine the local culture and traditions and (2) clashes between foreign investors and some members of the local elite (Leonard, 1980:461). Staley (1979:198–99) states that poor countries often have a difficult time assimilating the value structures and business methods associated with foreign investments. This especially may be true when the investment occurs in more modern sectors of the host economy, such as manufacturing. Vernon (1977:53–54) and Rothgeb (1984a:12–13) note that the advertising associated with investments in manufacturing fosters new conceptions of social relations, and Richardson (1978:4) sees foreign manufacturing firms as introducing a consumption orientation to societies in which most of the people cannot afford such a life-style. In each case, a higher probability of dissatisfaction and conflict is created.

Friction between foreign investors and the local elite emanates from the resentment that local nationalists, intellectuals, and businessmen feel toward what they see as foreign exploitation (Vernon, 1971:197; Moran, 1978:93–94). Moran (1974:10, 180) maintains that such conflict will focus especially on mining firms, which are seen as particularly exploitative, and where host vulnerability is low. Such is notably the case in wealthier countries, where the foreign contribution to resource extraction may be perceived as easily replaced (see the discussion in Chapter 2). Sklar (1975:176) also depicts extraction enterprises as contributing to domestic political tensions. Thus, mining investments foster friction and increase the likelihood of political conflict in the host country.

In summary, the liberalizing impact of multinational corporations occurs as a result of the increased resources that foreign activities bring. The specific projected effects are a stronger host government and more social reforms over time. In addition, foreigners are seen as laying the foundation for higher levels of domestic political conflict. In general, liberal theorists do not discuss foreign investments as encouraging the use of repression or as creating the sort of social atmosphere that makes the use of repression unavoidable.

THEORETICAL REFINEMENTS

The above arguments represent a diverse set of views that may be used as conceptual foundations for mapping out a precise picture of how foreign investment may be expected to affect the political and social climate in underdeveloped host societies. One may begin by noting that authors from each of the four schools of thought share the view that the relationship between the multinational corporation and the host government is competitive and conflictual. Important sources of tension are seen as stemming from local nationalism, which fosters some degree of xenophobia, and from a natural sense of resentment of foreign domination and exploitation on the part of local political leaders. For example, asymmetrical alliance theorists regard multinational corporations as seeking to enfeeble local local governments in order to reduce the potentially untoward consequences that would stem from a government capable of regulatory action. Symmetrical theorists also see conflict, with the government and the corporation each fighting to ensure that its own interests are advanced. The same is true of those who depict the corporation as having a malevolent influence, for the local government is seen as basing much of its policy behavior upon the need to counter the possibility of foreign domination. Finally, liberal theorists view the corporation as an object of local suspicion and argue that such circumstances cloud host government–corporate relations. In each case, to the extent that cooperation exists between foreign investors and host governments, whether as a part of an alliance or otherwise, it is depicted as occurring only because of the expectation of mutual benefits, not because any actor in the relationship wishes to behave charitably.

Hence, there is general agreement that the effects of the multinational corporation on local politics occurs within a competitive atmosphere. In such a framework, the relative strength of the actors in the relationship is a key to the type of outcomes one might expect. As has been noted previously, the resources available to actors and the intensity of involvement in their association with one another are important elements for determining the degree to which asymmetries in strength exist. However, there are more. Among the most vital from a government's point of view is its ability to rely upon the people for support (Morgenthau, 1973:135; Spanier, 1978:157–58; Jones, 1985:252–53). A government that is overly dependent upon foreign interests and that therefore is not legitimate, severely reduces the probability that it will be able to rely upon this support, and it places itself, or allows itself to be placed, in a precarious position. This is especially the case if the government allows the foreigners to enfeeble it.

If one assumes that governments will not choose to place themselves at risk if they can avoid doing so, then one may conclude that they will not submit willingly to control by foreigners. Augmenting this refusal to submit are the forces of nationalism and the resentment of foreign domination mentioned above. Thus, one may expect the government to be concerned with its relationship with the people it rules and with how the multinational presence affects this relationship, resisting the creation of circumstances that would turn the people against it unless there are significant countervailing benefits.

An important question revolves around the circumstances under which such resistance might occur and its consequences. Answering this involves considering how foreign corporations are likely to view the local political and social environment and their relationships with host governments.

For the corporation, a central consideration should be the type of operations it has in the host country, because this variable should affect both the degree to which the firm will need to involve itself in the host society and the vulnerability of the firm to local political vicissitudes. One would expect corporations engaged in manufacturing and in resource extraction to have particularly divergent perceptions of the local scene. The results from previous research indicate that manufacturing firms are more affected by the circumstances found in the host state because they rely on the local market for sales, they maintain extensive contacts with local firms that operate as suppliers and distributors, they require access to large numbers of local workers, and they need access to foreign exchange both to import the inputs needed to operate factories and to export profits (Reuber, 1973:37, 151–52; Vernon, 1977:10–11; Richardson, 1978:36–38; Caporaso, 1980:615; Frieden, 1981:407–13).

In contrast, mining operations generally are much more insulated and have fewer contacts with the host society. As mentioned in the previous chapter, such corporations tend to concentrate in small enclaves, with their primary interest centering on extracting resources for international markets (Vernon, 1971:196; Pinelo, 1973:12–13; Sklar, 1975:25; Mahler, 1981:273). The need for local involvement is small. Local labor requirements generally are not as great as is the case with manufacturing firms, and potential labor difficulties are kept to a minimum through the payment of wages that are above the local norm (Vernon, 1971:181–85; Reuber, 1973:174–75; Barnet and Muller, 1974:170; Cardoso and Faletto, 1979:169). Moreover, the concentration of mining firms upon international markets instead of local markets reduces the need for local involvement (Caporaso, 1980:615). In light of these considerations, it would appear that multinational corporations engaged in resource extraction would have few incentives to play an especially significant role in local politics.

Remaining outside the political realm is difficult, however, because mining operations are by their very nature controversial. As was discussed in Chapter 2, resource extraction projects usually are perceived as exploitative (see Pinelo, 1973:12–13; Vernon, 1977:149; Mahler, 1981:273). Under these conditions, it is unlikely that the host government would identify closely with foreign investors and cater to their wishes. Such behavior on the part of the government simply would drive a wedge between it and the people, thereby placing the government in a less secure position just to please foreigners for whom political leaders harbor a basic antipathy. These are hardly the sort of significant countervailing benefits mentioned above.

Consequently, there is little reason to believe that higher levels of foreign investment in mining will be associated with greater repression on the part of the host government. Instead, one might expect the government to seek to use the foreign corporate presence in mining to buttress its standing among the people. This may be accomplished by using the mining operations to obtain revenues to initiate programs of reform that appear to benefit the people. There are several reasons to believe that the government might behave this way. The first is that, as Dolan et al. (1982:391–92) point out, governmental decision makers place a very strong emphasis upon the goal of economic well-being for their society. For the most part, in underdeveloped societies economic well-being is translated as meaning development and growth. Indeed, the pressures for rapid development that are brought to bear on the government in underdeveloped societies are tremendous (Rothstein, 1977:112; Duvall and Freeman, 1981:112; Frieden, 1981:413). One means for handling these pressures and for enhancing the legitimacy of the government is to promote reforms designed to convince the people that the government is acting in their best interests (Rothgeb, 1986b:133–34). Of course, such reforms require the expenditure of money, and mining operations, which governmental leaders perceive as exploitative, may be regarded as a natural source of capital. Pinelo (1973), Moran (1974), and Sklar (1975) report that Peruvian, Chilean, and Zambian officials used resource extraction projects in their countries in just this way.

A second reason for expecting the government to build its support among the people is that, as Gereffi (1978:280) found, host governments often seek to limit foreign corporate activities in the host society by rallying the people to oppose the corporation. Reforms designed to help the people should make it easier for the government to pursue such a course. A final reason is derived from the scapegoating results in the preceding chapter, where it was found that governments use mining investors' home states as targets to blame for social ills in the host country. Given such foreign policy behavior toward the home state, it would seem reasonable to expect that the firm itself would be treated in a similar fashion and would be forced to contribute funds for local social improvements.

Thus, there are incentives for the host government to use foreign mining enterprises to promote reforms designed to aid the people. These incentives should be especially strong in very poor countries that are dependent upon investments from a single foreign national source. The dependence and poverty of such countries may render the government's position particularly precarious: dependence, by leading to the possible appearance of a government in league with foreign interests from a dominant developed state, and poverty, by creating an insufficient resource base for the government either to promote the development and the reforms needed to satisfy the people's aspirations and to enhance the government's legitimacy or to hold on to power through the use of coercion. These forces should result in both a xenophobic backlash against domination and an attempt to promote reform and lessen repression to demonstrate that the government is not a tool of foreign interests and is able to deliver in the area of development.

Foreign mining investments may be seen as a source of revenue for promoting reform. Mahler (1981:288) found that resource extraction projects enhance the revenues available to host governments. The sale on international markets of the bulk of the products that they mine means that such firms especially may be a source of the foreign exchange that is required to purchase many of the foreign-made inputs and to acquire the foreign consultants that often are needed to put reforms into effect (Rothgeb, 1986b:140). In very poor societies the impact of this increase in foreign exchange should be great and should be felt almost immediately, because the sale of commodities on foreign markets should begin as soon as the firm sets up operations. One might also expect these effects to continue over time for, as was discussed in Chapter 2, with the passage of time the host state's perception of vulnerability to foreign mining operations declines, and the host government will demand an increasingly larger share of corporate profits as compensation for allowing the firm to do business (Vernon, 1971:57; Moran, 1974:passim). The implementation of reforms should reduce the latent conflict found in the state and thereby lower the level of political conflict (see Jackson et al., 1978:631).

As far as wealthier Third World states are concerned, foreign investments in resource extraction should have a minimal effect upon the promotion of reform because the revenues and foreign exchange that they contribute to the local scene should be of a much more marginal significance than is the case in very poor societies. In wealthier countries, the primary social impact of mining corporations should revolve around the perception that such investments are exploitative. The belief that extraction projects take advantage of the host country should ensure that these firms are the subject of a considerable amount of political controversy, with the disputes being greatest where the investments are from a single foreign national source and therefore may be perceived as a part of an attempt by a developed country to control the mineral heritage of the host state.

Hence, mining investments may be expected to have much different effects in societies at different levels of development. In poor societies that are very dependent, these investments should lead to more social reform, less repression, and less political conflict. In wealthier societies with investments from one foreign national source, there should be more political conflict and no effect on reform or repression.

The situation regarding manufacturing investments should be different. As was discussed earlier, manufacturing investments are usually perceived by host government officials as contributing more than are mining investments to local development. Moreover, the intensity of involvement of the corporation and the home state and the consequent vulnerability of the actors in the relationship are quite different when one considers manufacturing investments. In this sector, firms usually operate in capital-intensive industries that require constant infusions of foreign technology and entrepreneurial talent (Vernon, 1977:93; Cardoso and Faletto, 1979:xx–xxi; Evans, 1979:81). Thus, the foreign contributions to the host economy is much more difficult to replace, and the firm has much more bargaining leverage vis-à-vis the host government.

These conditions apply particularly in poor and more dependent societies, where the manufacturing sector is highly valued as a key to the progress necessary to cement the government's legitimacy and its hold on power, yet where this vital sector is still nascent. Under these circumstances, foreign manufacturing firms may be perceived favorably by the government and should have a consid-erable degree of potential leverage.

Whether the foreign manufacturing investors will seek to profit from these advantages is doubtful, however, for very poor societies have too little to offer such corporations to make it worthwhile for them to attempt to play a significant political role in the host country. As was mentioned in Chapter 2, the markets in such states are of marginal value and the labor pool is questionable (see Rothgeb, 1986a:128–29). Consequently, on the whole, manufacturing investors may be expected to have relatively small stakes in poor countries. As a result, manufacturing investors will have little reason to play a large role in local politics, because the costs of playing such a role could nearly match or even exceed the possible benefits, given this small stake.

Instead, the greatest effect of manufacturing corporations should come from their contribution to a larger pool of available resources over time. The contribution to available resources should be most noticeable under two types of conditions. The first would exist in societies where the total stock of manufacturing investments is larger and where the increase in inflows of new investments from abroad and the reinvestment of corporate profits are relatively high. This expectation is based upon Rothgeb's (1984–85:30) finding that inflows of new investments and reinvestment of profits are positively associated with growth in the host state, thereby increasing the resource base (see also Bornschier et al., 1978:653–70; Bornschier, 1981:381–82; Jackman, 1982:191). The second set of conditions should be found in very poor and dependent societies, where the addition to the local resource base stemming from the activities in the manufacturing sector should be especially significant.

Increases in resources under these circumstances should add to the ability of the government to play a leading role in society, because it will provide the government with a greater pool of assets from which it may extract goods for managing society.[1] This ability of the government to play a greater role should result in (1) more social reforms as the government seeks to enhance its support among the people and (2) a reduction in political conflict as the greater reach of the government allows it to quell conflicts among groups that it previously could not control. The latter effect principally should be felt in very poor countries where the reach of the government is limited by the lack of resources. Each of these effects should only occur over time as the foreign manufacturing presence adds to resource availability.

In states at higher levels of development the impact of foreign manufacturing investments may be less pronounced. The greater wealth in these countries means a larger resource base and a more marginal contribution by the foreign firm to resource availability. Higher wealth in the host state also should create a different set of priorities as far as economic well-being is concerned and should mean less fear by the government that popular revolts may dislodge it from power. Whereas governments in poorer countries may be forced to implement reforms to build support among the people, those in wealthier societies may find this less necessary. Thus, incremental increases in resource availability in richer countries may not have a major impact on the introduction of social reform. At the same time, there is little reason to believe that the government would perceive it as sound social policy to turn its back on the people, for the people still may be regarded as a useful source of strength for controlling the reach of the foreign investors (see Gereffi, 1978:280).

It is in the area of political conflict that one might expect manufacturing investments to have the greatest effect in more developed states. The manufacturing sector may be seen as vital and on the leading edge of development in such countries. Hence, it should be jealously guarded, and a large foreign presence may be the subject of considerable suspicion, most notably when the investments are from a single foreign national source. Such a situation may be the source of tension, because, as was mentioned above, foreign investments in manufacturing tend to center in more advanced and sophisticated industries and therefore may be regarded as strategically situated in the host economy. As was indicated by the foreign policy results in Chapter 2, a large foreign presence in such an important position in the host economy is controversial and is perceived as a significant threat to local autonomy. The result should be higher levels of political debate and political conflict regarding the means for controlling and limiting the foreign presence.

SUMMARY AND CONTROL VARIABLES

The foregoing discussion is built around the basic assumption that multinational corporation–host government relations in underdeveloped countries are conflictual. As a result of this conflict, the relative strength of the corporation and the government are regarded as key factors for analyzing how foreign investment affects host country politics. Given this situation, it is assumed that the host government cannot ignore cultivating the support of the people and will be loathe to place itself in the hands of foreigners, relying upon the aid of foreign interests to remain in power. It is within this context that foreign investments are depicted as affecting the local political environment.

The specific effects of foreign investment on local politics are seen as being affected by two factors: (1) the sector in which the investment occurs and (2) the level of development and degree of dependence of the host state. When the host country is very poor and highly dependent, with high stocks from a single foreign national source, and when the foreign investments are in resource extraction, the expectation is that the stock of foreign investment will be (1) positively related to social reforms, (2) negatively related to repression, and (3) negatively associated with political conflict by way of the positive relationship with social reform. Mining investments in richer countries with a large stock from a single foreign national source should be the subject of considerable political controversy. Thus, the hypothesis is that in such states stocks of mining investments will be positively related to political conflict.

The expectations regarding manufacturing investments are different. In poor countries that are very dependent, it is posited that foreign investments will produce more resources over time, leading to a stronger government and to more social reform and less political conflict. In wealthier countries, the increase in resources from manufacturing investments should have less impact on reform and repression but should produce more political conflict when the investments are from a single foreign national source.

Finally, a high inflow of new foreign investments and reinvestment of profits in countries with higher stocks of investments in manufacturing should increase over time both the government's role in society and its ability to promote reform. This effect is expected to occur because of an increased availability of resources.

Before discussing the empirical analysis, the question of control variables must be addressed. As was the case in Chapter 2, a key factor that must be included in the analysis is resource availability. Within the present context, the resources found in the host state are of special significance. These are controlled for by using the same measure for population that was employed earlier.

THE RESEARCH DESIGN

The same basic research design employed in Chapter 2 is used here to investigate the effects of foreign investment upon four dependent variables: (1) the host government's role in regulating and managing society, (2) the government's pursuit of social reforms, (3) the government's use of repression against the people it rules, and (4) the level of domestic political conflict found in the host society. The first of these variables, governmental management of society (abbreviated GovMan), was measured as total central government expenditures divided by total gross domestic product (GDP) for the first year of each of the time periods examined (1967–69, 1970–72, 1973–75, 1976–78). The use of central government expenditures was based upon the assumption that managing a society requires the expenditure of money and that higher expenditures of money by the government indicate a greater role for the government as a regulator and manager. Weighting central government expenditures by GDP was based upon the further assumption that the size of a country would determine the efficacy of a given level of expenditures, with the effect being greater in smaller countries than in larger countries. Dividing by GDP was designed to provide a measure that accounts for this. As was the case in Chapter 2, all monetary values were measured in constant 1970 United States dollars (see note 10, Chapter 2).

Operationalizing the other three dependent variables required the use of another type of data. These variables represent the incidence either of differing types of governmental policy behavior (as in the case of the promotion of social reforms and the use of repression) or of particular types of social behavior (as in the case of political conflict). Thus, the measurement of these variables involves determining the frequency with which these sorts of governmental and social behavior occur. Monetary values of the sort used above provide no ready means for doing this. Events data from the COPDAB domestic data file, however, are well suited to this purpose. The COPDAB domestic file draws from the same

sources to cover the same countries and the same years as the COPDAB international data file that was used in Chapter 2 (see Azar, 1980:142–52; 1982;30–
36). The basic difference between the two files is that the domestic file codes
political and social events that occur within the countries in the data set, while
the international scale focuses upon foreign policy behavior. Hence, the COP-
DAB domestic file provides the researcher with a means for determining the
frequency with which specific types of political and social behavior occur within
particular countries. These are the sort of data required at present.

Within the COPDAB domestic file, events are coded on a 15-point scale, with
each point on the scale representing a different type and intensity of cooperation
and conflict. Social reform (Reform) was measured by using values 1, 2, and 3 on
this scale, which represent government programs such as creating health clinics
for the poor, enacting social security legislation, initiating agrarian reform, and
improving the distribution of income among the people. Repression (Repress)
was operationalized using values 11, 12, and 14, which denote such government
actions as restricting internal travel, imposing curfews, forbidding public meet-
ings, arresting opposition leaders, closing universities, imposing martial law, and
decreeing censorship. Finally, political conflict (PolCon) was measured by using
value 10 on the scale, which includes public demonstrations against the government, political strikes, the distribution of antigovernment propaganda, calls for
the resignation of governmental officials, and widespread criticism of government
policies. These points on the COPDAB scale conform closely to the conceptions
found in the literature of the variables that they are used to measure.

Computing the scores for each of these variables involved two steps. First,
the total frequency of each type of domestic behavior for each country was
summed separately for each time period. Second, this total was divided by the
total number of events of all types that were reported for each state for each
time period. The result was scores that represented the proportions of a country's
total events in each time period that involved reform efforts, repression, and
political conflict. This is the same basic procedure that was used in Chapter 2
for developing measures based on events data, with proportions being used to
avoid situations in which states with high total numbers of events automatically
have high scores, even though a relatively small percentage of their total events
may represent any particular type of behavior.

The dependent variables mentioned above were conceptualized as being affected by (1) the total stock of foreign investment in manufacturing and in mining
(TotInvMan and TotInvMin); (2) the interaction among the total stock of foreign
investment in manufacturing and in mining, a low level of development for the
host state, and a high proportion of investment from a single foreign national
source (LoDevel × HiConcen × TotInvMan and LoDevel × HiConcen x
TotInvMin); (3) the interaction among the total stock of foreign investment in
manufacturing and in mining, a high level of development for the host state,
and a high concentration of investment from a single foreign national source
(HiDevel × HiConcen × TotInvMan and HiDevel × HiConcen × TotInvMin);

and (4) the interaction between the total stock of investment in manufacturing and in mining and a high inflow of new investments and reinvestment of profits (Hi Flow × TotInvMan and HiFlow × TotInvMin). The control variable was total population. With the exception of the interaction variables for high flows, each of these variables was measured as was done in Chapter 2.[2]

Operationalizing the flows interaction term required first that flows be measured. As has been discussed by many previous researchers (Dolan and Tomlin, 1980:55; Jackman, 1982:188; Rothgeb, 1984b:1067; Rothgeb, 1984–85:12; Rothgeb, 1986b:144), direct measures of inflows of new investments and the reinvestment of profits that are broken down according to sectoral location are not available. As a result, it was necessary to employ an indirect measure based upon the change in the total stock of foreign investment over time. The procedure suggested by Jackman (1980:606; 1982:188) was used. Flows were calculated using the continuous growth formula discussed by Taylor and Hudson (1972:206):

Growth $= Ln(Vtn / Vt1) / n$

where

Ln = natural logarithm

Vtn = the value of the variable in the last year of the time period

$Vt1$ = the value of the variable in the first year of the time period

n = the number of years between $t1$ and tn

For the calculation of flows, Vtn was the value of total stocks in 1971 and Vt1 was the value of total stocks in 1967. It should be noted that measuring flows by comparing stocks at two different points in time provides one with an approximation of the amount of increase or decrease in the total size of the foreign presence over time. Such a change only partially reflects the flows and reinvestments that occur (see Rothgeb, 1986b:146). However, the dearth of data on direct investment flows leaves one with few alternatives to this sort of measure. For the most part, prior researchers who have examined flows have based their measure on the difference in stocks (see Bornschier et al., 1978; Dolan and Tomlin, 1980; Bornschier, 1981; Jackman, 1982; Rothgeb, 1984b, 1984–85, 1986b).

Constructing the flows interaction term required the use of a dummy variable to represent a high level of flows and reinvestments. This variable was created by assigning a value of 1 to all states with a flow that equalled or exceeded the median flow for all states in the data set and a value of 0 to all states with a flow that was below the median. The median was 0.015.[3] States assigned a value of 1 were regarded as having a high flow. Interaction terms were created by multiplying the total stock of foreign investment in manufacturing and in mining by this dummy variable.

Standard multiple regression analysis was used to assess the effects of the independent variables upon the dependent variables. Problems of the sort discussed in Chapter 2 relating to multicollinearity dictated the use of separate regression equations to examine the main effects of foreign investment and the effects of each of the interaction terms. Scatterplots of the bivariate relationship between each independent variable and each dependent variable also were examined as a check for nonlinear patterns of relationship. No such patterns were apparent.[4]

The reader might recall that the theoretical discussion posited both direct and indirect effects of foreign investments upon the dependent variables. Using the manufacturing variables as an example, the first set of equations tested for the direct effects of foreign investment upon governmental management:

(1) $GovMan = a + b1TotInvMan + b2Pop + e$

(2) $GovMan = a + b1LoDevel \times HiConcen \times TotInvMan + b2Pop + e$

(3) $GovMan = a + b1HiDevel \times HiConcen \times TotInvMan + b2Pop + e$

(4) $GovMan = a + b1HiFlow \times TotInvMan + b2Pop + e$

Other sets of identical equations tested for the direct effects of foreign investment upon social reform, repression, and political conflict, with each of these dependent variables being substituted individually for GovMan in the above equations.

The indirect effect of foreign investment on the dependent variables was assessed by including the presumed intervening variable as an independent variable together with foreign investment in the same equation. Nie et al. (1975:386–87) and Asher (1976:11–20) discuss this use of regression analysis for examining indirect effects of the sort investigated here. Thus, the effects of foreign investment upon social reform by way of a prior impact on governmental management involved first examining the results for the direct effect on governmental management obtained from the above equations and then assessing the results obtained from the following set of equations:

(5) $Reform = a + b1TotInvMan + b2GovMan + b3Pop + e$

(6) $Reform = a + b1LoDevel \times HiConcen \times TotInvMan + b2GovMan + b3Pop + e$

(7) $Reform = a + b1HiDevel \times HiConcen \times TotInvMan + b2GovMan + b3Pop + e$

(8) $Reform = a + b1HiFlow \times TotInvMan + b2GovMan + b3Pop + e$

Similar equations, substituting Repress and PolCon for Reform as dependent variables, were utilized to examine the claims found in the literature that foreign investment induces repression and political conflict by way of a prior effect that produces a greater (or lesser) role for the government in managing society (see the alliance and malevolent influence arguments outlined above).

Two other indirect effects also were examined. These involved situations where foreign investment affected political conflict by way of a previous effect upon reform and affected repression as a result of an effect upon political conflict. These indirect effects were analyzed using the above equations that assess the direct effects of foreign investment on the intervening variables and two sets of equations that investigate the effects of both foreign investment and the inter-vening variable on the dependent variable. The equations for examining the indirect effect of reform on political conflict were as follows:

(9) $PolCon = a + b1TotInvMan + b2Reform + b3Pop + e$

(10) $PolCon = a + b1LoDevel \times HiConcen \times TotInvMan + b2Reform + b3Pop + e$

(11) $PolCon = a + b1HiDevel \times HiConcen \times TotInvMan + b2Reform + b3Pop + e$

(12) $PolCon = a + b1HiFlow \times TotInvMan + b2Reform + b3Pop + e$

The following are the equations for the indirect effect of political conflict upon repression:

(13) $Repress = a + b1TotInvMan + b2PolCon + b3Pop + e$

(14) $Repress = a + b1LoDevel \times HiConcen \times TotInvMan + b2PolCon + b3Pop + e$

(15) $Repress = a + b1HiDevel \times HiConcen \times TotInvMan + b2PolCon + b3Pop + e$

(16) $Repress = a + b1HiFlow \times TotInvMan + b2PolCon + b3Pop + e$

The effects of mining investments were examined using equations analogous to those above, except that TotInvMin and the relevant mining interaction terms were substituted for TotInvMan and the manufacturing interaction terms.

The reader is reminded that synchronic and time-lagged analysis are employed just as they were in Chapter 2. It should be noted that the measure for flow of foreign investment did not conform precisely to the 1967–69 time period that was used as the base for the measurement of the independent variables. For this variable the problem of data availability required that the measurement be based upon values for 1967 and 1971.[5] When the indirect effects of foreign investment were assessed, the measures for the control variables added to the equation (GovMan, Reform, and PolCon) were lagged to coincide with the measures of the dependent variables.

RESULTS

The results for the effects of foreign investments on governmental management are in Tables 3.1 and 3.2. Table 3.1 reveals that stocks of foreign investment

Table 3.1
Foreign Investments in Manufacturing and Central Government Expenditures

Time Lag	TotInvMan	LoDevel x HiConcen x TotInvMan	HiDevel x HiConcen x TotInvMan	HiFlow x TotInvMan	Pop	R^2	N
No Lag	-.07				-.17	-.01	
		-.09			-.16	-.01	55
			.10		-.12	-.01	
				.20	-.09	.02	
Three Year	.06				.00	-.03	
		.06			.00	-.03	65
			.11		.00	-.02	
				.15	.00	-.01	
Six Year	.19				-.07	.02	
		.24			-.08	.04	65
			-.07		-.12	-.02	
				.20	-.08	.02	
Nine Year	.30*				-.04	.07	
		.34**			-.07	.10	65
			-.06		-.12	-.02	
				.47****	-.02	.20	

*p<.05
**p<.01
****p<.0001

Table 3.2
Foreign Investments in Mining and Central Government Expenditures

Time Lag	TotInvMin	LoDevel x HiConcen x TotInvMin	HiDevel x HiConcen x TotInvMin	HiFlow x TotInvMin	Pop	R^2	N
No Lag	-.18				-.22	.02	
		-.19			-.16	.02	53
			-.10		-.18	.00	
				.02	-.16	-.01	
Three Year	-.08				-.07	-.03	
		-.09			-.05	-.02	59
			-.03		-.05	-.03	
				-.02	-.05	-.03	
Six Year	-.14				-.20	.01	
		-.05			-.16	-.01	59
			-.05		-.17	-.01	
				-.10	-.18	.00	
Nine Year	-.14				-.21	.01	
		-.09			-.17	.00	59
			-.10		-.19	.00	
				-.03	-.18	-.01	

Table 3.3

Foreign Investments in Manufacturing and Social Reform

Time Lag	TotInvMan	LoDevel x HiConcen x TotInvMan	HiDevel x HiConcen x TotInvMan	HiFlow x TotInvMan	Pop	R^2	N
No Lag	.20				-.04	.01	
		.22			-.07	.02	55
			-.25		-.15	.03	
				-.09	-.11	-.02	
Three Year	-.13				-.17	.00	
		-.02			-.14	-.01	65
			.02		-.13	-.01	
				.00	-.13	-.01	
Six Year	.00				.08	-.03	
		.03			.08	-.03	65
			-.16		.05	.00	
				-.15	.05	.00	
Nine Year	.28*				.03	.04	
		.28*			.03	.05	64
			.05		.01	-.03	
				.35**	.06	.09	

*p<.05
**p<.01

in manufacturing are positively related after nine years to governmental management both in countries with high flows and countries that are poor and have a high level of investment from a single foreign national source. At the same time, manufacturing investments had no effect on wealthier countries with a high concentration of investments. The absence of an effect also is found in Table 3.2 for mining investments. These are precisely the sorts of effects that were outlined above in the revised theoretical discussion. Manufacturing investments appear to increase over time the resource base in very poor and dependent countries and in countries with higher flows, providing the government with a greater ability to play a role in society.

The direct effects of manufacturing and mining investments on social reform are illustrated in Tables 3.3 and 3.4. The manufacturing results in Table 3.3 indicate that increased resource availability in poor and dependent countries and in societies with high flows lead to a greater effort to promote reform after nine years. The results for mining investments in Table 3.4 reveal a similar pattern for flows, with the interaction term for high flows being positively related to reform after nine years. The synchronic results also show that the interaction term for poor countries with a high concentration is positively related to reform.

The results in Tables 3.5 and 3.6, which include the level of governmental management as a control variable in the regression equation, reveal that the effects on social reform are complex. Adding GovMan to the equation has no effect upon the relationship between the interaction terms representing high flows and the incidence of social reform. In each case, a significant positive relationship

Table 3.4
Foreign Investments in Mining and Social Reform

Time Lag	TotInvMin	LoDevel x HiConcen x TotInvMin	HiDevel x HiConcen x TotInvMin	HiFlow x TotInvMin	Pop	R²	N
	-.31*				-.22	.06	
No		.30*			-.11	.07	53
Lag			-.23		-.16	.03	
				-.08	-.13	-.02	
	-.03				-.13	-.02	
Three		-.13			-.14	.00	59
Year			.00		-.13	-.02	
				-.07	-.13	-.01	
	-.06				.13	-.01	
Six		.26			.15	.05	59
Year			-.13		.12	.00	
				.09	.17	-.01	
	-.04				.04	-.03	
Nine		.25			.04	.03	58
Year			.00		.05	-.03	
				.32*	.12	.07	

*p<.05

Table 3.5
Foreign Investments in Manufacturing and Social Reform with a Control for Governmental Expenditures

Time Lag	TotInvMan	LoDevel x HiConcen x TotInvMan	HiDevel x HiConcen x TotInvMan	HiFlow x TotInvMan	Pop	GovMan	R²	N
	.22				.00	.25	.06	
No		.24			-.03	.26	.07	55
Lag			-.28		-.12	.27	.09	
				-.14	-.09	.27	.03	
	-.13				-.17	.05	-.01	
Three		-.02			-.13	.05	-.03	65
Year			.02		-.13	.04	-.03	
				-.01	-.13	.05	-.03	
	-.06				.10	.30*	.05	
Six		-.05			.11	.30*	.05	65
Year			-.14		.08	.28*	.06	
				-.22	.08	.33**	.09	
	.25				.07	.12	.05	
Nine		.24			.04	.11	.04	64
Year			.06		.03	.20	-.01	
				.33*	.07	.04	.08	

*p<.05
**p<.01

Table 3.6

Foreign Investments in Mining and Social Reform with a Control for Governmental Expenditures

Time Lag	TotInvMin	LoDevel x HiConcen x TotInvMin	HiDevel x HiConcen x TotInvMin	HiFlow x TotInvMin	Pop	GovMan	R^2	N
No Lag	-.28				-.18	.18	.07	
		.35*			-.07	.29	.13	53
			-.21		-.13	.12	.05	
				-.09	-.10	.22	.01	
Three Year	-.02				-.13	.11	-.02	
		-.12			-.13	.10	-.01	59
			.00		-.12	.11	-.02	
				-.07	-.13	.11	-.02	
Six Year	.00				.21	.43***	.16	
		.28*			.22	.45***	.24	59
			-.11		.20	.43***	.17	
				.13	.25*	.44***	.18	
Nine Year	.02				.11	.36**	.08	
		.28*			.10	.38**	.16	58
			.03		.11	.36**	.08	
				.36**	.19	.40**	.21	

*p<.05
**p<.01
***p<.001

is found, indicating that in states with higher levels of investments in either manufacturing or in mining a high flow adds resources that lead directly to the promotion of more social reform.

The findings in Table 3.6 for poor countries with a high concentration of mining investments conform closely to the expectations outlined above. The immediate positive relationship found in Table 3.4 is present when there is a control for governmental management. The six- and nine-year-lagged results reveal that governmental management masks the relationship between mining investments and reform, with there being a positive association between these variables at any given level of governmental management. A similar masking effect appears in Table 3.5, where government management masks the synchronic negative relationship between reform and manufacturing investments in richer countries with investments from one foreign source.[6]

The results for manufacturing investments in poor countries with a high concentration of investment from one source present an interesting picture. First, the significant positive effect found in Table 3.3 declines when governmental management is included in the equation. Second, when governmental management is included in the manufacturing equations it is not related to reform after nine years, but when the same variable is included in the mining equations a fairly strong positive association is found. This pattern suggests that the apparent effect of governmental management upon reform after nine years is a product

Table 3.7
Foreign Investments in Manufacturing and Political Conflict

Time Lag	TotInvMan	LoDevel x HiConcen x TotInvMan	HiDevel x HiConcen x TotInvMan	HiFlow x TotInvMan	Pop	R^2	N
	-.25				-.03	.02	
No		-.29*			.01	.05	55
Lag			.24		.10	.02	
				.09	.07	-.03	
	-.21				.07	.03	
Three		-.22			.10	.03	65
Year			.11		.15	.00	
				-.05	.12	-.01	
	-.16				.19	.05	
Six		-.26*			.19	.09	65
Year			.33**		.29	.13	
				.02	.23	.02	
	-.23				.13	.05	
Nine		-.26*			.15	.05	64
Year			.25		.23	.06	
				-.07	.17	.01	

*p<.05
**p<.01

of manufacturing investments and that the effects found for manufacturing investments in poor countries with a high concentration of investments are indirect and are the product of a prior positive relationship with governmental strength. The results in both Tables 3.5 and 3.6 indicate that governmental strength has a positive association with reform after six years that is independent of the effects of foreign investment.

The direct and indirect effects of foreign investment in manufacturing upon political conflict are illustrated in Tables 3.7 to 3.9. The results in Table 3.7 indicate that for the subset of wealthier countries with investments from one foreign source, manufacturing investments are positively related to political conflict after six years. This relationship holds even with the controls for governmental management and reform found in Tables 3.8 and 3.9. Including governmental management in the equation, as in Table 3.8, indicates a positive synchronic relationship, while the inclusion of reform in the equation, as in Table 3.9, reveals a positive relationship after nine years, implying that these two variables have masking effects similar to those found above. Manufacturing investments also have an indirect positive synchronic relationship by way of their negative association with reform (see Table 3.5), which in turn is negatively related to political conflict (see Table 3.9). Thus, among this subset of countries, manufacturing investments consistently are associated with higher levels of political conflict.

The findings in Table 3.7 imply that there is a negative relationship between manufacturing investments and political conflict for the subset of poorer countries

Table 3.8

Foreign Investments in Manufacturing and Political Conflict with Controls for Governmental Expenditures

Time Lag	TotInvMan	LoDevel x HiConcen x TotInvMan	HiDevel x HiConcen x TotInvMan	HiFlow x TotInvMan	Pop	GovMan	R^2	N
	-.27*				-.09	-.35**	.13	
No		-.32*			-.05	-.37**	.17	55
Lag			.28*		.05	-.36**	.14	
				.17	.03	-.37**	.09	
	-.20				.07	-.19	.05	
Three		-.21			.10	-.19	.06	65
Year			.13		.15	-.22	.03	
				-.02	.12	-.20	.01	
	-.11				.17	-.28*	.11	
Six		-.20			.17	-.25*	.14	65
Year			.31**		.25*	-.28*	.19	
				.08	.20	-.32*	.10	
	-.22				.13	-.02	.04	
Nine		-.26			.15	.00	.06	64
Year			.24		.23	-.07	.05	
				-.04	.17	-.06	-.01	

*p<.05
**p<.01

with investments from one foreign source. When governmental management is added to the equation in Table 3.8, however, the longer-term negative relationship disappears. The same happens to the synchronic effects found when reform is in the equation, as in Table 3.9, suggesting that the relationship between manufacturing investments and political conflict is largely spurious among this subset of countries.

The results for the effects of mining investments on political conflict in Tables 3.10 to 3.12 reveal the same basic pattern as found for manufacturing investments. Among the subset of wealthier countries with investments from a single foreign source, mining investments are consistently associated with higher levels of political conflict. These effects are both direct, standing up even when governmental management and reform are controlled for, as in Tables 3.11 and 3.12, and they are indirect, via the synchronic negative relationship with reform, which is negatively associated with political conflict. For the subset of poorer countries with investments from one foreign source, the only relationship found is a negative indirect synchronic effect, where mining investments are related to higher levels of reform, which is associated with less conflict. On the whole, these results conform quite closely to the projection found in the revised theoretical discussion.

The final set of findings pertains to the relationship between foreign investment and repression. The results for manufacturing investments are in Tables 3.13 through 3.15. These tables reflect a general negative synchronic relationship

Table 3.9
Foreign Investments in Manufacturing and Political Conflict with Controls for Reform

Time Lag	TotInvMan	LoDevel x HiConcen x TotInvMan	HiDevel x HiConcen x TotInvMan	HiFlow x TotInvMan	Pop	Reform	R²	N
	-.16				-.04	-.43**	.19	
No		-.20			-.02	-.41**	.20	55
Lag			.13		.03	-.43**	.18	
				.05	.01	-.45***	.17	
	-.25				.02	-.25*	.08	
Three		-.22			.07	-.23	.07	65
Year			.11		.12	-.22	.03	
				-.05	.09	-.22	.02	
	-.16				.20	-.24	.09	
Six		-.26*			.21	-.23	.13	65
Year			.30*		.30*	-.19	.15	
				-.02	.24	-.24	.06	
	-.18				.15	-.17	.07	
Nine		-.21			.16	-.16	.08	64
Year			.26*		.24	-.23	.10	
				.00	.19	-.22	.04	

*p<.05
**p<.01
***p<.001

between repression and manufacturing investments both for poor and for wealthier countries with investments from one source. No longer-term effects are found. The relationship for wealthier countries is found in Table 3.13 and is unaffected by the controls for governmental management and political conflict that are introduced in Tables 3.14 and 3.15. The relationship among poorer countries appears only in Table 3.15, where there is a control for political conflict, indicating that among this group of states political conflict has a masking effect on the relationship between manufacturing investments and repression.

The association between mining investments and repression is pictured in Tables 3.16 to 3.18. The effects of mining investments are centered in poor countries with investments from one foreign source, much as was projected in the theoretical discussion above. Within this subgroup of states, the synchronic and three-year-lagged results show that higher stocks of investments are associated with lower levels of repression, implying that host governments seek to build support among the people and enhance their legitimacy by reducing the use of force as an instrument of policy.

The implications of the above results are discussed in the following section.

CONCLUSIONS

A review of the empirical results from this chapter reveals that the theoretical expectations found in the revised discussion were generally supported. The ef-

Table 3.10
Foreign Investments in Mining and Political Conflict

Time Lag	TotInvMin	LoDevel x HiConcen x TotInvMin	HiDevel x HiConcen x TotInvMin	HiFlow x TotInvMin	Pop	R^2	N
	.49***				.20	.18	
No		-.19			.03	.00	53
Lag			.46***		.13	.17	
				.00	.03	-.04	
	.09				.13	-.02	
Three		-.14			.09	.00	59
Year			.20		.15	.02	
				-.14	.08	-.01	
	.33*				.28	.10	
Six		-.13			.18	.01	59
Year			.42**		.27	.17	
				.00	.19	.00	
	.43**				.27	.16	
Nine		-.16			.15	.01	58
Year			.43***		.23	.17	
				-.21	.10	.03	

*$p < .05$
**$p < .01$
***$p < .001$

fects of multinational corporations upon local political and social behavior appear to occur within an atmosphere of conflict between the host government and the foreign firm and vary both according to the sectoral location of the investment and according to the level of development and the degree of domination of the host society.

Among poorer countries with the bulk of their foreign investments from one foreign national source, the foreign presence apparently is perceived suspiciously and is regarded as a source of revenues that the government may use to tighten its grasp on power by buttressing its position among the people, especially when the investments are in the mining sector. The empirical results show that larger levels of mining investments located in countries of this sort are associated with more social reform, less repression, and less political conflict. The higher level of social reform, which is found both early on and consistently over time, may be interpreted as representing a government's attempts to use foreigners who are perceived as exploiting the host society (as mining investors often are) to their advantage, promoting reforms to appease the people's demands for social progress. The lower level of repression is a product of the same trend and may reflect the government's attempt to pursue a noncoercive strategy based upon the extension of reforms that are financed in part by the corporation. This desire, however, is not permanent, for it disappears after six years. The effect on political conflict, which is a product of the prior effect on reform, is ephemeral, indicating that while the introduction of social reforms has a very immediate effect on

Table 3.11
Foreign Investments in Mining and Political Conflict with Controls for Governmental Expenditures

Time Lag	TotInvMin	LoDevel x HiConCen x TotInvMin	HiDevel x HiConcen x TotInvMin	HiFlow x TotInvMin	Pop	GovMan	R^2	N
	.44**				.13	-.29	.25	
No		-.26			-.04	-.41**	.14	53
Lag			.43**		.07	-.31*	.25	
				.02	-.02	-.36*	.07	
	.07				.12	-.25	.03	
Three		-.17			.08	-.27*	.06	59
Year			.20		.13	-.25	.07	
				-.14	.07	-.26*	.05	
	.28*				.21	-.34**	.20	
Six		-.14			.12	-.38**	.15	59
Year			.40***		.21	-.36**	.29	
				-.04	.12	-.38**	.13	
	.41**				.25	-.11	.15	
Nine		-.18			.12	-.18	.03	58
Year			.42**		.21	-.13	.17	
				-.24	.06	-.19	.05	

*p<.05
**p<.01
***p<.001

political conflict, the collective memory of the people is short, and social improvements only alleviate the tendency toward conflict for a brief period of time.

Future research should be directed toward determining why the easing of repression is only temporary and why reforms only ameliorate conflict for a short period, as well as how foreign investment plays a role in the process. At present, it is suspected that these are related, with repression reappearing as political conflict increases. For its part, the return of political conflict may occur because controversies in host societies most probably reflect basic social cleavages that are not eliminated by reforms. Social reform may put a damper for a short time on the conflict resulting from these cleavages, but they may be expected to reappear later on as a source of trouble.

The effects of manufacturing investments in poorer and more dominated countries were somewhat different. Here it was expected that the government would be less inclined to feel hostility toward the foreign investor and to regard such investments as a source to tap for revenues. Instead, the host government was expected to welcome such investments, perceiving them as bringing valuable inputs to help spur development. The results supported this view. The synchronic results revealed that manufacturing investments are associated with less repression, indicating that such investments may prompt the host government to begin adopting a more noncoercive policy early on. The results also imply that manufacturing investments increase the local resource base over approximately a

Table 3.12

Foreign Investments in Mining and Political Conflict with Controls for Reform

Time Lag	TotInvMin	LoDevel x HiConcen x TotInvMin	HiDevel x HiConcen x TotInvMin	HiFlow x TotInvMin	Pop	Reform	R^2	N
No Lag	.36**				.11	−.42***	.33	
		−.04			−.03	−.51***	.22	5
			.36**		.06	−.44***	.35	
				−.03	−.04	−.52****	.22	
Three Year	.08				.11	−.20	.01	
		−.17			.06	−.22	.03	5
			.20		.12	−.19	.04	
				−.15	.05	−.21	.02	
Six Year	.31*				.31*	−.27*	.16	
		−.05			.22	−.27*	.07	5
			.39**		.30*	−.24	.22	
				.03	.23	−.29*	.07	
Nine Year	.42**				.27*	−.20	.18	
		−.12			.15	−.18	.03	5
			.43***		.24	−.21	.20	
				−.16	.12	−.16	.04	

*p<.05
**p<.01
***p<.001
****p<.0001

decade and that the result is a greater role for the host government in managing society, a development which in turn leads to more social reforms. It was projected in the theoretical discussion that the increased level of social reform would lower the level of political conflict, as was the case with mining investments. The empirical analysis did not reveal such a pattern; however, one might speculate that longer time lags (of perhaps a decade and a half) are needed to investigate such an effect, for the impact on political conflict was expected to result from a prior effect on social reform, and that effect only appeared in the nine-year-lagged results.

The theoretical discussion projected that the basic effects of foreign investment upon wealthier countries with investments from one foreign national source would center around political conflict. In the mining sector, conflict would center on the perception that foreigners were exploiting the host country. In the manufacturing sector, the increased conflict would result from the fear that foreigners were playing too great a role in a vital part of the host economy. Both expectations were supported by the empirical results, with foreign investments being related consistently over time with higher levels of political conflict.

Two unexpected effects also were uncovered for manufacturing investments. Both were immediate, appearing in the synchronic results. The first was the tendency for manufacturing investments to lead to less social reform. The second was the tendency toward less repression. A possible explanation for these results

Table 3.13
Foreign Investments in Manufacturing and Repression

Time Lag	TotInvMan	LoDevel x HiConcen x TotInvMan	HiDevel x HiConcen x TotInvMan	HiFlow x TotInvMan	Pop	R²	N
	-.40**				-.18	.12	
No		-.27			-.10	.04	55
Lag			-.36*		-.15	.09	
				-.11	-.10	-.02	
	-.14				-.04	-.01	
Three		-.19			-.02	.01	65
Year			-.05		-.01	-.03	
				.07	.00	-.03	
	-.07				-.09	-.02	
Six		.02			-.07	-.02	65
Year			-.22		-.11	.02	
				-.14	-.10	-.01	
	-.16				-.06	-.01	
Nine		-.08			-.03	-.03	64
Year			-.21		-.06	.01	
				-.24	-.06	.03	

*p<.05
**p<.01

Table 3.14
Foreign Investments in Manufacturing and Repression with Controls for Governmental Expenditures

Time Lag	TotInvMan	LoDevel x HiConcen x TotInvMan	HiDevel x HiConcen x TotInvMan	HiFlow x TotInvMan	Pop	GovMan	R²	N
	-.38**				-.14	.27*	.18	
No		-.24			-.06	.28*	.10	55
Lag			-.39**		-.11	.34**	.19	
				-.17	-.07	.33*	.07	
	-.15				-.04	.06	-.03	
Three		-.20			-.02	.06	-.01	65
Year			-.05		-.01	.06	-.04	
				.07	.00	.04	-.04	
	-.07				-.09	.00	-.04	
Six		.02			-.07	-.02	-.04	65
Year			-.22		-.12	-.03	.01	
				-.15	-.10	.01	-.02	
	-.14				-.06	-.08	-.02	
Nine		-.04			-.04	-.11	-.03	64
Year			-.22		-.08	-.13	.01	
				-.23	-.06	-.01	.01	

*p<.05
**p<.01

Table 3.15
Foreign Investments in Manufacturing and Repression with Controls for Political Conflict

Time Lag	TotInvMan	LoDevel x HiConcen x TotInvMan	HiDevel x HiConcen x TotInvMan	HiFlow x TotInvMan	Pop	PolCon	R^2	N
	-.46***				-.19	-.25	.17	
No		-.34*			-.10	-.24	.08	55
Lag			-.34*		-.15	-.07	.08	
				-.09	-.09	-.14	-.02	
	-.16				-.04	-.10	-.02	
Three		-.22			-.01	-.11	.00	65
Year			-.04		.00	-.06	-.04	
				.07	.02	-.06	-.04	
	-.09				-.05	-.18	-.01	
Six		-.03			-.04	-.17	-.02	65
Year			-.18		-.09	-.10	.01	
				-.14	-.06	-.16	.00	
	-.18				-.05	-.09	-.02	
Nine		-.09			-.02	-.06	-.04	64
Year			-.21		-.07	.01	-.01	
				-.24	-.05	-.05	.01	

*p<.05
***p<.001

Table 3.16
Foreign Investments in Mining and Repression

Time Lag	TotInvMin	LoDevel x HiConcen x TotInvMin	HiDevel x HiConcen x TotInvMin	HiFlow x TotInvMin	Pop	R^2	N
	-.19				-.15	.00	
No		-.35**			-.09	.10	53
Lag			-.12		-.11	-.02	
				.10	-.06	-.02	
	-.06				.03	-.03	
Three		-.29*			.00	.05	59
Year			-.05		.03	-.03	
				.12	.06	-.02	
	-.03				-.05	-.03	
Six		-.06			-.04	-.03	59
Year			-.05		-.05	-.03	
				.23	.00	.02	
	-.08				.00	-.03	
Nine		-.01			.02	-.04	58
Year			.00		.02	-.04	
				-.19	-.02	.00	

*p<.05
**p<.01

Table 3.17
Foreign Investments in Mining and Repression with Controls for Governmental Expenditures

Time Lag	TotInvMin	LoDevel x HiConcen x TotInvMin	HiDevel x HiConcen x TotInvMin	HiFlow x TotInvMin	Pop	GovMan	R^2	N
	-.14				-.09	.27	.06	
No		-.31*			-.05	.24	.14	53
Lag			-.09		-.06	.29*	.05	
				.10	-.02	.29*	.05	
	-.04				.03	.14	-.03	
Three		-.28*			.02	.12	.05	59
Year			-.05		.04	.15	-.03	
				.12	.07	.15	-.02	
	-.02				-.04	.02	-.05	
Six		-.06			-.04	.02	-.05	59
Year			-.05		-.05	.02	-.05	
				.24	.02	.05	.01	
	-.09				-.03	-.11	-.04	
Nine		-.02			.00	-.10	-.04	58
Year			-.02		.00	-.10	-.04	
				-.20	-.05	-.13	-.00	

*p<.05

Table 3.18
Foreign Investments in Mining and Repression with Controls for Political Conflict

Time Lag	TotInvMin	LoDevel x HiConcen x TotInvMin	HiDevel x HiConcen x TotInvMin	HiFlow x TotInvMin	Pop	PolCon	R^2	N
	-.15				-.14	-.07	-.02	
No		-.39**			-.08	-.21	.13	53
Lag			-.07		-.10	-.11	-.03	
				.10	-.06	-.14	-.02	
	-.06				-.06	.00	-.05	
Three		-.30*			.01	-.05	.04	59
Year			-.06		.03	.00	-.05	
				.12	.06	.01	-.04	
	.02				.00	-.14	-.03	
Six		-.08			-.01	-.15	-.03	59
Year			.00		-.01	-.14	-.03	
				.24	.03	-.14	.02	
	-.08				.00	.00	-.05	
Nine		-.02			.02	-.03	-.05	58
Year			.00		.02	-.02	-.05	
				-.20	-.02	-.06	-.01	

*p<.05
**p<.01

is that host governments in wealthier states expect a larger manufacturing presence to allow them to pursue the sort of noncoercive strategy just mentioned, using revenues from the foreign presence to finance social reform. The additional resources derived from the foreign corporate presence may be only marginal, however, as was discussed above, and the end result, may be a temporary decline in the implementation of social reform. Future research in another context should address this possibility carefully.

In conclusion, the results from this chapter, together with those from Chapter 2, suggest that it is useful to regard the multinational corporate presence in Third World countries as involving an asymmetrical interdependent relationship between the foreign firm and the host government. It is within this context that the effects on local political and social processes occur. This is the approach that shall be employed in Chapter 4, which seeks to examine the effects of foreign investment on growth in the host economy.

NOTES

1. It should be noted that the expectation that a higher flow and reinvestment of profits will increase the government's role in society, and by extension that a lower flow will do the reverse, runs counter to Duvall and Freeman's (1983:579) contention that a low flow will force an increased governmental role. The reason for these diverse expectations is found in the assumptions that underlie the theoretical discussions. Duvall and Freeman appear to base their argument on the assumption that underdeveloped host governments are able to draw upon a pool of unused resources to replace the shortfalls that occur when multinational corporations fail to invest at the preferred (higher) level. The assumption herein is that in underdeveloped countries the desire for rapid development dictates that all available resources be plowed into the attempt to produce progress and to convince the people that advances are occurring and that, as additional resources become available, they are added to the effort. If the latter assumption is correct, then the sort of relationship posited in this analysis should hold, and a high flow and reinvestment in countries with a larger manufacturing presence should be associated with a larger governmental role over time.

2. The reader is reminded that the analysis was replicated using varying cutoff points when creating the dummy variables and the interaction terms, as described in Chapter 2, note 11. In each case, the results were the same as are reported.

3. In addition to using the median, the dummy variable was constructed using .020 and .025 as cutoff points, and the analysis was replicated with interaction terms based upon these values. In each case, the results were the same as those that are reported.

4. The reader is reminded that this comment should not be taken to mean that all of the relationships were linear (see Chapter 2, note 12).

5. Previous empirical research has been based upon this same substitution (see Dolan and Tomlin, 1980; Jackman, 1982; Rothgeb, 1984b; 1984–85; 1986b). Thus, while the design is not exactly as one would prefer, the practice from earlier research indicates that this substitute is acceptable.

6. See Nie et al. (1975:305) for a discussion of masking effects.

4

Foreign Investment and
Host Country Growth

In this chapter attention shifts from the political and social effects of foreign investment to the impact that such investments purportedly have upon growth. In moving to this topic, the analysis focuses upon the most often discussed and contentious of the effects of foreign investment upon underdeveloped countries. The disputes surrounding this subject parallel the arguments discussed in earlier chapters. A key difference between the debates in those chapters and the one considered here resides in the amount of previous empirical research that has been devoted to investigating the topic. As mentioned earlier, the foreign policy and political and social effects discussed in Chapters 2 and 3 have been researched only sporadically in the past. The impact of foreign investment on growth, however, has been the subject of much previous work.

Despite the large quantity of research, the results have been relatively inconclusive thus far, and the discussion continues. Chase-Dunn (1975:720–26), Portes 1976:61–82), McGowan and Smith (1978:183–85), and Jackman (1982:176–82) point out the widespread disagreement that exists in the literature and note that there are varying schools of thought as to whether foreign investment promotes or retards economic growth and development. This debate indicates the need for further study designed to address the conditions under which foreign investment either contributes to or retards growth and the specific mechanisms by which these effects are felt.

The goal in this chapter is to explore systematically the relationship between foreign investment and growth in Third World countries. Four basic types of problems associated with the research to date shall be addressed. The first is the lack of sector specific analysis. Virtually all theorists regard foreign investments as having differing effects upon the host state that vary according to the sector in which the investments are located. The results from earlier chapters in this book strongly reinforce these arguments. Yet, despite calls from Ray (1973:11), McGowan and Smith (1978:187), and Mahler (1981:270), almost none of the available research considers this aspect of the problem.

The second and third problems are methodological. One is that time-lagged analysis of the sort used in the preceding chapters is required to investigate claims regarding the short-term and long-term effects of foreign investment on growth that are frequently found in the literature. As Rothgeb (1984–85:12–13) notes, such analysis rarely appears in past research. Another problem is the need to examine the potential indirect routes by which foreign investments supposedly affect growth. The analysis of such indirect effects is essential if one is to acquire a complete understanding of how foreign investments affect host country growth and if one is to move beyond mere speculation as to which of several competing reasons are responsible for any relationships that are found. Past research almost uniformly fails to consider the specific indirect impacts of foreign investments upon growth.

The final problem is conceptual. There is a basic need to consider the validity of the logic and assumptions that underpin much of the research to date. Much of the discussion of growth is built upon the sorts of conceptions regarding the domestic effects of foreign investment that were outlined in Chapter 3. Consequently, an examination of the relationship between foreign investment and growth provides an opportunity to consider further these differing conceptual pictures of the domestic effects of foreign investment.

The approach used in this chapter shall mirror the one used in past chapters. The literature regarding foreign investment and growth shall be outlined briefly. Following this, theoretical and methodological refinements shall be considered, and empirical analysis will be addressed.

FOREIGN INVESTMENT AND GROWTH

An examination of previous work on foreign investment reveals several sets of expectations regarding the potential effects on growth. One group of views is based upon conceptions of the sort that serve as the foundation of the thinking of asymmetrical alliance theorists, with foreign investments being seen as making no positive contribution to growth. A second follows the tack of symmetrical alliance analysis, regarding foreign investments as contributing to imbalance growth in more developed Third World countries. The third takes a malevolent influence approach, regarding foreign investments as creating social and economic problems that harm host country prospects for growth. Finally, there is a liberal group that depicts foreign investment as enhancing the host state's capital and resource availability, its ability to manage efficiently, and its technological competence, thereby creating the conditions for growth. Each of these views is outlined in the following pages.

Asymmetrical Alliance

As has been outlined in earlier chapters, the asymmetrical alliance conception is built around the notion that multinational corporations are an instrument used for controlling underdeveloped countries. Working together with the local elite, the corporation is seen as dominating targeted countries. The evidence from Chapters 2 and 3 indicates that if such mastery does exist, it does not extend to the realm of foreign policy or to the area of domestic political and social decision making.

Such findings do not rule out the possibility of the sort of hegemonic relationship that asymmetrical theorists have in mind, however, for the primary purpose of the alliance may not be focused on affecting local foreign or domestic policy but may reside instead in the desire to attain important economic goals. Dos Santos (1971:226) clearly has this in mind when he defines the dependence found in the asymmetrical alliance as "a situation in which the economy of certain countries is conditioned by the development and expansion of another economy to which the former is subjected." Galeano (1971:211) is even more explicit in arguing that the control of the local economy is a fundamental goal of the multinational corporation, stating that "the importance of the new phenomenon (the multinational corporation) . . . (is) the capture of markets from within."

Foreign domination reportedly is attained through control of the "commanding heights" of the local economy and through an alliance with a local elite that needs foreign support to remain in power (see the discussion in Chapters 2 and 3). Dos Santos (1971:230) describes the situation as one where "foreign capital retains control over the most dynamic sectors of the economy." This allows foreign corporations to regulate growth and development in the host country and only to permit such economic development as is "geared toward the needs of the dominant economies" (Bodenheimer, 1971:158). Galeano (1971:221) argues that "the great multinational corporations . . . obviously hold the keys to the (host country) economy."

The basic goal of the multinational corporation is the maintenance of an international division of labor. Within this division of labor, the less developed countries of the periphery serve as raw material suppliers and consumers of finished goods, while the developed states in the center process raw materials and supply finished goods for consumption (Galtung, 1971:86). The dominant position of the corporation in the periphery and its alliance with the local elite allow the foreigners to perpetuate this division of labor by channeling local efforts into the exploitation of natural resources and away from the development of manufacturing capabilities (Bodenheimer, 1971:159; Rubinson, 1976:643; Chase-Dunn and Rubinson, 1977:468). Baran (1957:197) argues that "the main task of [corporate] imperialism in our time . . . [is] to prevent . . . the economic development of underdeveloped countries." Doing this creates an unequal relationship that is beneficial to the developed center in which "development of parts of the system occur at the expense of other parts'' (Dos Santos, 1971: 226).

Maintaining an international division of labor implies the need to retard growth in the manufacturing sector of the host state. The key to preventing this growth is found in the effect of foreign investment on the local accumulation process. Galeano (1971:215) describes the surplus capital produced in the host economy as ''drained off by foreign interests.'' The siphoning off of local capital is a product of the excessive repatriation of profits by foreign corporations (Bodenheimer, 1971:157; Brundenius, 1972:200; Magdoff, 1976:217). As Dos Santos (1971:226–27) states, ''an export of profits and interest . . . carries off part of the surplus generated domestically.'' The result of repatriation is a reduced ability to marshal the domestic investment needed to promote growth, leading to an inability to develop, particularly in areas such as manufacturing, where high amounts of capital availability are required.

In addition to the damage done by repatriation, capital accumulation is stunted by the export orientation of the accumulation process, which is built around commodity sales (Senghaas, 1975:262). This export orientation allows the corporation to control both the pricing and marketing of the goods upon which capital accumulation is based. Dos Santos (1971:229) notes that ''only in rare instances does foreign capital not control . . . the marketing of these products.'' Such domination is seen as allowing the corporation to set prices that clearly are insufficient to support local development efforts.

In doing this, the foreigners are aided and abetted by a local elite that wishes to prevent the rise of a local commercial class that might serve as its competitor for local domination. Brundenius (1972:195) describes the multinational corporation as assisting the local elite by

greatly limiting the possibilities of a 'national bourgeoisie' in the . . . underdeveloped world . . . The small independent native entrepreneur is confronted with the alternative of either being absorbed by international capital or being out-competed and joining the ranks of the proletariat.

Thus, foreign investments are seen as having significant stunting effects on growth, especially in the manufacturing sector. Since the promotion of an international division of labor that forces underdeveloped countries to remain resource producers is regarded as a key goal of foreign interests, investments in resource extraction may be regarded as the central agent in this process. Foreign investments in manufacturing are also seen as playing a role, however, for they ensure that local manufacturing enterprises are coopted, bought out, or driven out of business. As was noted in previous chapters, one might expect that the probability that foreign investment plays such a role is highest in countries that are easily dominated; that is, where the host country is very poor and where there is a high level of investment that is predominantly from a single foreign national source.

Symmetrical Alliance

The discussion in Chapter 3 noted that symmetrical alliance theorists regard multinational corporations in manufacturing that operate in wealthier Third World countries as part of a coalition that includes the host government and local entrepreneurs. One of the basic purposes of this coalition is the promotion of rapid growth and development in the host economy. Encouraging this growth is seen as having benefits for each member of the coalition. The local government is able to increase its grasp on power and its legitimacy by providing the local population with an apparently ever-expanding pool of resources. While the benefits derived from these resources are seen by symmetrical theorists as distributed very unevenly, a continuing pattern of growth fosters an atmosphere of progress that works to the government's advantage (Cardoso and Faletto, 1979:167). Economic expansion is regarded as aiding foreign investors and local entrepreneurs by increasing the base from which they draw their profits.

Three specific types of mechanisms are regarded as accounting for this growth. The first is the reinvestment of profits and the inflow of new investments and technology by multinational corporations. Inflows of investments and reinvestments of profits increase capital availability, thereby promoting growth, while foreign technology concentrates in industries where domestic entrepreneurs are unable to operate efficiently, which leads to an expanded scope of economic activity and growth (Evans, 1979:119, 203). The maintenance of a substantial inflow of capital and technology and a reinvestment of profits over time is regarded as a fundamentally important contribution of foreign corporations to the symmetrical alliance and as a key source of its continuing political influence with the host government (Fagen, 1978:294; Cardoso and Faletto, 1979:161–63; Evans, 1979:213–73).

The second mechanism connecting foreign investment to growth stems from the effects of these investments upon domestic investment. Evans (1979:101–62) sees a large multinational corporate presence as encouraging local capitalists to engage in businesses designed to complement the foreign activities. The result is a higher level of domestic investment and a greater degree of economic growth.

The third mechanism centers around the presumed effect of foreign investment upon the role the local government plays in the economy. As Evans (1979:43–50) discusses, the government is a central player in the accumulation and investment process in underdeveloped countries. A large multinational role in the host economy is seen both as spurring the government to play a more active role in managing local resources to produce greater growth and as providing the government with the means to pursue such strategies.

The growth resulting from these activities is seen as imbalanced, for it is sector specific, occurring only in manufacturing. Manufacturing is the arena where foreign investors and local entrepreneurs stand to earn their greatest profits and where the government has the best opportunity to create the aura of progress that it considers vital. More traditional sectors, such as agriculture, are neglected

(Evans, 1979:95). This neglect results in lower rates of growth and production. Slower growth is a product of at least two factors. One is the diversion of local resources toward the favored manufacturing sector (Cardoso and Faletto, 1979:164). Included in this diversion are governmental funds and the investments of local entrepreneurs. Another is the channeling of local labor away from agriculture to provide the large urban proletariat required by the factories upon which progress is based. Only a few of these displaced agricultural workers, however, actually find employment in industry. The bulk are forced to seek jobs in the lower-paying service sector. As Evans (1979:95) notes, "most of those who moved out of agriculture found jobs not in industry, but in the tertiary sector."

In each case, foreign investment is regarded as a key to the creation of a climate that emphasizes progress and defines it in terms of growth in industry, which leads to the lack of attention to agriculture. Hence, a large foreign presence in manufacturing is regarded as associated with greater growth in manufacturing, the sector in which the foreigners are able to obtain the greatest profits, and lower growth in areas such as agriculture, which, while they may benefit the population of the host society as a whole, promise few rewards for foreigners.

Malevolent Influence

Theorists who regard foreign investments as having a malevolent impact upon the host country generally hold the view that any positive effects for foreign investments upon growth are ephemeral and are unevenly distributed across sectors. For the most part, these possible positive effects are regarded as short-term and are seen as centering on more modern sectors of the host economy (see Hveem, 1973:334: Sunkel, 1979:216; Duvall and Freeman, 1981:102; Mahler, 1981:275).

Three different reasons for the short-term nature of this growth are found in the literature. One is attributed to the varying effects of stocks and flows of foreign investment upon growth. Bornschier et al. (1978:653–70) argue that higher flows are associated with higher short-run growth, while higher stocks are related to lower long-term growth. Rubinson (1977:4) provides a similar argument.

Bornschier (1981:381–82) and Bornschier and Chase-Dunn (1985:81–82) discuss the rationale for these expectations. Flows produce higher growth early on because they add to the available pool of investment capital in the country. This increase produces growth, for greater investment is one of the major determinants of higher economic growth (see Papanek, 1973: 121; Chenery and Syrquin, 1975:23). Over the long- run, however, higher stocks of foreign investment are regarded as having a dampening effect on growth. Bornschier and Chase-Dunn argue that the reason for this is that foreign investments, especially in the manufacturing sector, primarily are designed to enhance the corporation's ability to market its products in the host country. Over time, as the size of the foreign corporate holdings increase (that is, as stocks in manufacturing become large), local markets are saturated, and the potential for future increases in profits decreases. When this happens, the "corporation, as a private growth and profit-seeking institution, will look for new investment opportunities within its world-wide operations" (Bornschier and Chase-Dunn, 1985:81). In other words, as time passes, higher levels of stocks in manufacturing are associated with lower levels of flows into the host economy, and the rate of growth falls as the sum of available capital thereby declines.

A second reason for the expectation that growth is ephemeral relates to the effects of foreign investment upon host government behavior. As was discussed in Chapter 3, some theorists regard a large foreign role in the host economy as leading to attempts at counterbalancing by the host government. Such behavior is seen as most notable when the foreign investment is in the manufacturing sector (Cardoso and Faletto, 1979:165; Duvall and Freeman, 1981:113). Counterbalancing involves increased government expenditures intended to create a locally controlled industrial base to ensure that a significant proportion of the local manufacturing sector remains under local control. Pumping governmental funds into the local economy in this manner stimulates growth. If the government's ability to pursue this course of action is tied closely to the continued infusion of foreign funds into the host economy (as the results from Chapter 3 imply) and if the inflow of such funds and the reinvestment of profits falls over time in the manner discussed above, then the ability of the government to pursue this strategy for promoting growth would be severely impaired.

The third reason for expecting only short-term growth has to do with the impact foreign investments are regarded as having upon domestic investments. Foreign investments are discussed as having three basic long-term detrimental effects upon domestic investment. One is a product of the relationship between the multinational corporation and locally owned businesses. Foreign corporations are seen as overwhelming and destroying their local competitors, resulting in a lower level of domestic investment (Barnet and Muller, 1974:138–39). A second impact results from the promotion of a consumption orientation among the elite in underdeveloped countries. In poorer societies with scarce resources, increased consumption by members of the upper class subtracts from the resources required for investment and hurts growth over time (Barnet and Muller, 1974:172–84; Bornschier and Chase-Dunn, 1985:81–82). A final deleterious effect results from the repatriation of the profits that foreign investors secure from their local op-erations. The practice of repatriating profits is depicted as soaking up domestic capital and transporting it abroad, which results in lower domestic investment and a substantially reduced ability to promote growth (Barnet and Muller, 1974:140–41; Pinto, 1974:109; Mahler, 1980:31).

As noted previously, many authors regard the effects of foreign investment as uneven. The above patterns predominantly are attributed to investments in manufacturing (see Rothgeb, 1984–85:7; 1986b:140). Bornschier (1981:383) argues that higher levels of investment in more modern sectors, such as manufacturing, are accompanied by lower levels of growth in more traditional sectors, such as agriculture. Barnet and Muller (1974:170) and Evans and Timberlake (1980:533) explain that foreign investments in manufacturing create higher-paying jobs than are available to the bulk of the population, especially those who work in agriculture. This prompts a diversion of labor away from agriculture, as rural laborers migrate to seek more lucrative employment in industry. The result is lower growth in the agricultural sector due to the loss of labor. Hence, the expectation is that foreign investment in manufacturing is negatively associated with agricultural output.

Foreign investments in resource extraction are described as having similar effects upon the agricultural sector. Barnet and Muller (1974:166–70), Sklar (1975:120), Sunkel (1979:216), and Mahler (1981:286) describe such investments as driving up the local wage scales and drawing agricultural workers to mining towns in search of higher-paying jobs, leading to lower growth in the agricultural sector. In addition to this, these investments are seen as contributing little to growth in other sectors because they remove important natural resources at the very low prices set by the multinational firms that control international markets, thereby harming the ability to accumulate the investment capital required to promote growth (Evans, 1971:330–32).

The Liberal View

The fourth conception of the relationship between foreign investment and growth is built around the notion that foreign inputs bring essential ingredients that often are missing in underdeveloped countries. Chief among these ingredients are the capital, technology, and entrepreneurial talent that host underdeveloped countries sorely need in order to promote growth. The introduction of these necessary components to growth are most notable when the investments are in the manufacturing sector. Ranis (1976:99) notes that creating growth requires much larger quantities of capital than often are available in poor countries and that foreign investments may make an important contribution to overcoming this problem. Beyond this, I. Frank (1980:31) sees multinational corporations as bringing to the local scene technology that enhances growth by increasing the efficiency of industrial production.

In addition to these direct effects, foreign investments are regarded as having an indirect impact. Vernon (1971:171) states that "these foreign owned subsidiaries were much more than conduits of foreign capital; they were mobilizers of local resources." Domestic resources are depicted as being stimulated in four ways. The first involves putting nonused resources to work. As Vernon (1971:155) puts it, "one wave of consequences can usually be seen in the mobilizing of some added local funds . . . [T]hese [often] are acquired . . . by rescuing them from idleness" A second is the product of the stimulation of economic activity by local entrepreneurs who act as suppliers and distributors for the foreign corporations (Reuber, 1973:37, 151–52; Vernon, 1977:142; I.

Frank, 1980:31). A third stimulant is a product of the dissemination over time of the efficient foreign product techniques and management styles to local businesses (Moran, 1978:87). Finally, foreign profits from local operations are pictured as leading to reinvestments and to higher tax receipts, which brings on greater domestic investments and higher government expenditures. In each case, foreign investments enhance local resource availability, either through higher domestic investment or through higher government expenditures, and the end product is a higher rate of growth in the manufacturing sector.

Chenery and Syrquin (1975:53) and Rothstein (1977:173) argue that investments in the manufacturing sector have similar positive effects upon growth in agriculture. Foreign investments in modern sectors are discussed as increasing over time the availability of production techniques and machinery that may be used to increase agricultural productivity. Moreover, such investments also are depicted as enhancing growth in the host state's transportation and communications facilities, which in turn aid the agricultural sector by easing marketing problems.

Similar views are found regarding the effects of foreign investments in mining. Heilbroner (1963:110–11), Diaz-Alejandro (1970:322), and Vernon (1971:45–47) see extraction investments as allowing a country to tap resources that otherwise would have been untouchable, making capital available for the development of infrastructure (transportation and communications) and manufacturing. As development occurs in these sectors, it may then lead to growth in other areas, such as agriculture.

Thus, liberal theorists tend to see foreign investments as having benefits that lead to growth in all areas of the host economy.

SUMMARY OF VIEWS AND RESEARCH RESULTS

The above schools of thought represent a diverse set of expectations regarding the relationship between foreign investment and growth in poor host countries. A careful consideration of each set of views suggests several specific mechanisms by which foreign investment purportedly affects growth. Asymmetrical alliance theorists center their attention on growth in manufacturing and discuss three basic paths connecting foreign investment to growth. The first posits slower growth as a result of the lower domestic investment that is a product of the repatriation of profits. The second depicts slower growth as coming from a lower level of domestic investment created by a higher stock of foreign investment in mining, and the third sees a higher stock of investment in manufacturing as stunting domestic investment and thereby leading to lower growth. These effects should be most prevalent among poorer and more dominated countries.

Symmetrical alliance theorists focus upon different sets of mechanisms that affect countries at higher levels of development. One discusses flows of foreign investment both as leading directly to higher growth in manufacturing and to greater growth in this sector via a prior effect that increases domestic investment.

A second pictures stocks in manufacturing as increasing domestic investment and governmental expenditures, both of which lead in turn to greater growth in manufacturing. A third portrays depressed agricultural growth as occurring because stocks in manufacturing increase domestic investment and governmental expenditures and decrease the labor force engaged in agriculture.

A key distinguishing feature of the thinking of malevolence theorists is found in the contention that the effects of foreign investment shift over time. Early on, higher flows of foreign investment are seen as contributing to higher growth in manufacturing both directly and indirectly as a result of a positive relationship with domestic investment. Over time, however, foreign investments are seen as having detrimental effects on growth that are the product of several different types of indirect effects. One sees stocks in manufacturing as lowering flows and as producing lower domestic investment and governmental expenditures, each of which leads to lower manufacturing growth. Another depicts the repatriation of profits as harming domestic investment and thereby lowering manufacturing growth. A third sees stocks in both manufacturing and in mining as decreasing the agricultural labor force and creating lower growth in agriculture. Finally, stocks in mining are regarded as harming growth in manufacturing by lowering domestic investment.

Liberal theorists produce a fourth set of causal expectations. Stocks in manufacturing are pictured as directly enhancing growth in manufacturing and as creating the basis for higher growth as a product of positive relationships with domestic investment and governmental expenditures. Flows also are regarded as leading directly to higher manufacturing growth and to greater domestic investment, which in turn results in more manufacturing growth. Growth in the agricultural sector is portrayed as being aided by foreign investment in both manufacturing and in mining. Stocks in manufacturing have a direct effect and an impact that results from a positive relationship with growth in transportation and communications. Stocks in mining have effects that occur due to positive associations with growth in manufacturing and in transportation and communications.

These theoretical projections have been only partially investigated in the empirical research to date. Thorough outlines of the existing literature are available in Bornschier et al. (1978:653–70), Rothgeb (1984–85:4–10), and Bornschier and Chase-Dunn (1985:80–90, 131–41); hence, only a brief summary is required here. According to Bornschier et al. and Bornschier and Chase-Dunn, the evidence to date supports the arguments made by what are labeled herein as malevolence theorists. Flows were reported in recent research as being positively associated with growth in studies by Bornschier et al. (1978:673), Dolan and Tomlin (1980:53), Bornschier (1981:385), Jackman (1982:191), and Rothgeb (1984–85:30; 1986a:141–48), and stocks were found to be negatively related to growth in research reported by Bornschier et al. (1978: 673), Gobalet and Diamond (1979: 427–33), Dolan and Tomlin (1980:53), and Bornschier (1981:385). Moreover, Bornschier and Chase-Dunn (1985:131–41) argue that systematic research supports the arguments that foreign investment lowers the rate of domestic investment, decreases the role the government plays in society, and reduces the agricultural labor force. Thus the case made by malevolence theorists would seem sound.

There are several problems, however, with this picture. The first is that it does not include the findings from the research of several scholars. For example, Jackman (1982:191) found no relationship between stocks and growth; nor did McGowan and Smith (1978:220) in their study of African nations. Rothgeb (1984–85:31) cast doubt upon the long-term effects of stocks with the finding that there is a small, but immediate, negative relationship between stocks of foreign investment in manufacturing and growth in manufacturing. In addition, Mahler's (1980:87–90) research revealed that higher stocks are associated with higher rates of growth, and Rothgeb (1984a:11) found that stocks of U.S. foreign investment in manufacturing, transportation and communications, and domestic trade generally were positively associated with growth in underdeveloped countries.

Beyond this, research pertaining to the effects of foreign investment upon intervening variables indicates that malevolence arguments are not as well supported as suggested above. Bornschier and Chase-Dunn (1985:136) discuss only a procedure that "indirectly" tests this relationship. Rothgeb (1986a:139) found no long-term relationship between stocks of foreign investment in manufacturing and flows of foreign investment in a more direct test. An examination by Rothgeb (1986b:150) of the effect of repatriation upon domestic investment revealed that the profits from the operations of foreign corporations were positively associated with domestic investment, not negatively related, as Bornschier and Chase-Dunn suggest. Finally, the empirical support for the hypothesis that there is a negative relationship between stock of foreign investment and governmental expenditures is based largely upon research reported by Rubinson (1977:14) and Gobalet and Diamond (1979:428–29). In neither case, however, are the results statistically significant. Moreover, Mahler (1981:288) found a positive relationship between stocks of foreign investment in mining and governmental revenue and the results from Chapter 3 also indicate that the expectation of a negative relationship between state strength and foreign investment is inaccurate.

A second set of problems pertains to research procedures and methodology. First, there is the need to employ time-lagged analysis when examining the short- and long-term effects of foreign investment upon growth. For the most part, synchronic analysis has been employed in the research to date, with stocks and flows being measured for the same periods of time. When this is done, problems are created.[1] One is that the analyst cannot be sure which variable is the cause and which is the effect. As Heise (175:5) and McGowan (1975:66) note, causes precede effects (see the research design discussion in Chapter 2). With the use of synchronic analysis, it is difficult to determine whether foreign investment produces (or retards) growth or vice versa. For instance, it is entirely plausible that a high rate of growth attracts higher flows of foreign investment, instead of being produced by these flows. Indeed, Diaz-Alejandro (1970:324) argues that over the years, foreign investment has been attracted to those Latin American states that have recorded the highest growth rates. Evans' (1979:76) research on Brazil supports this possibility, as does Lim's (1983:210) recent cross-national work. A clearer determination of the effects of stocks and flows of foreign investment may be obtained through the use of time-lagged analysis of the sort used in Chapters 2 and 3.

Another difficulty is associated with the need to use sector-specific analysis. Clearly, one cannot adequately test any of the above arguments without looking at the effects of foreign investment in different sectors of the host economy. Each set of arguments projects very specific effects that vary across sectors. Interestingly enough, however, very little of the research to date resorts to sector-specific analysis. Chase-Dunn (1975) examined the effect of the total profits earned by foreign investors upon growth in agriculture, manufacturing, and mining. Szymanski (1976) investigated the effects of U.S. investments in manufacturing on growth in Latin America. Evans and Timberlake (1980) studied the effect of total stock of foreign investment on employment in the service sector. Mahler (1981) analyzed the effects of stocks in agriculture, manufacturing, and mining on social distribution. Only Rothgeb (1984a; 1984–85) has considered the effects of total stocks and flows of foreign investment on growth in several sectors of the host economy. Yet, as useful as this work may be, it suffers from the failure to consider the specific sort of mechanisms that connect foreign investment to growth. Consequently, the results only allow one to speculate as to which of several competing reasons are responsible for the effects found.

This points at the final methodological problem associated with the research to date. That is, there has been a failure to seek to determine the specific means by which foreign investment affects growth. Several possible connections between foreign investment and growth were outlined in the above discussion. A more complete understanding of the role played by foreign investments in underdeveloped societies makes it imperative that these possibilities be examined carefully. In calling for such analysis, Rothgeb (1986b:131) notes that while problems of data availability do exist, it still is imperative to seek to discover which of the possible routes by which foreign investment may exert an effect are the most plausible.[2]

A final difficulty that must be addressed is conceptual. The centerpiece of the malevolent argument is that corporate penetration only proceeds up to a point and eventually is reversed, creating an outflow of capital from host underdeveloped countries. That is, early on, stocks increase as a result of continual inflows and reinvestments. As time passes, however, local economic activity is insufficient to sustain the level of penetration previously achieved, inflows and reinvestments cease, and an outflow begins. This argument rests upon at least five assumptions. The first is that multinational corporate executives are unable to gauge the host state economy accurately enough to avoid overpenetration and overproduction. The second is that corporate leaders will regard a period of slack consumption as permanent and will be ready to abandon markets that they initially judged favorably enough that a considerable stock of investment was built up. The third is that markets in underdeveloped countries, especially consumer markets, are easily saturated. The fourth is that there are no countervailing effects of foreign investment on the local economy that may compensate for any tendency toward slack consumption (such as increased local investment or the expansion of local exports). Finally, it is assumed that the host government either will view a corporate pullout with equanimity or will be incapable of taking action to prevent such behavior.

Each of the above assumptions is questionable. Work by Reuber (1973:107–10), Fieldhouse (1978:345–79), I. Frank (1980:43–56), Lowe (1981: 151), and Rothgeb (1986a:130, 148) casts strong doubt upon the first two assumptions. These authors found both that corporate executives plan carefully to avoid overpenetration (and generally do well with such forecasting) and that they are reluctant to leave markets in which they have a large stake and that are regarded as promising. The fourth assumption is undermined by Rothgeb's (1986b:167) findings that foreign investment is associated both with higher domestic investment and with more favorable terms of trade for the host state, and the fifth assumption is brought into question by the results from Chapters 2 and 3, which indicate that host underdeveloped governments do watch corporate behavior closely and seek to control this behavior when it appears to have a potential for adversely affecting the host society.

Possible support for the third assumption is more difficult to assess. The potential for saturation should be associated closely with the level of development of the host society. In poor countries, one might expect saturation to occur rather easily. The probability would seem small, however, that there would be attempts to pursue a consumption-oriented multinational corporate strategy in such a context. In wealthier countries, saturation may be more problematic, for resource availability is greater and the economy may be able to support an ongoing process of growth in consumption. Moreover, Vernon (1976:43) argues that multinational corporate penetration in more developed states generally occurs in an atmosphere in which consumption markets already are fairly well established and that in such a context foreign corporate goods tend to substitute for some locally made consumer goods. Hence, there is reason to doubt the market saturation assumption.

These arguments and methodological problems point to the need for a reconsideration of the effects that foreign investment may be expected to have on growth in underdeveloped countries. The following section addresses this task.

THEORETICAL REFINEMENTS

A reconsideration of the impact of multinational corporations upon growth in host states may begin with the same fundamental assumption that served as the foundation for the analysis in Chapter 3. This is that the relationship between the foreign firm and the host government basically is competitive. By this it is meant that each actor has a specific set of goals that, on the whole, holds only for that actor. For multinational firms, the overriding goal is the maximization of profits. Numerous authors, representing views that span the spectrum from those who are extremely critical of foreign investments, such as Bodenheimer (1971:157), Dos Santos (1971:228), and Magdoff (1976:217), to those who are more sympathetic, such as Vernon (1971:172), Reuber (1973:105), and Kindleberger (1979:94), agree that this is the basic goal pursued by multinational corporations. As far as the host government is concerned, the key domestic goal is to produce economic growth in order to enhance its legitimacy, augment its hold on power, and provide benefits for the people (see Rothstein, 1977:112; Duvall and Freeman, 1981:112; Frieden, 1981:413; Krasner, 1981:200; Dolan et al., 1982:391–92; Rothgeb, 1986b:133).

A competitive relationship also means that each actor is preoccupied with achieving its own goals and is not particularly interested in the objectives held by other actors. Thus, it is assumed that the multinational firm is not overly concerned with host country growth, except insofar as such growth ensures the profitability of its operations, and the host government is not worried about corporate profits, except as they may contribute to local economic expansion. In other words, neither type of actor altruistically seeks to aid the other in achieving its objectives. Such aid as is given therefore either will be incidental, occurring as a product of the pursuit of each actor's own goals, or will result from the ability of one actor to coerce the other into cooperating.

Within this context, the attainment of goals and the ability to force the other actor to contribute should depend on the relative strength of each actor. In other words, the effects of foreign investment should be tied closely to the relative political clout wielded by each actor. As was discussed in Chapters 2 and 3, the relative strength of the actors in an ongoing relationship with one another is affected by their resource availability and intensity of involvement in the relationship (see Dolan et al., 1982:389). In general, as has been discussed previously, this means that poorer and more dependent underdeveloped states are in difficult situations when dealing with multinational corporations, for their poverty both reduces their resource pool and increases their needs from the external environment, resulting in a higher intensity of involvement.

One other factor must be considered when assessing the relationship between the host government and the foreign firm: the sovereign reach of the host state. As Claude (1971:23) and Morgenthau (1973:307–11) discuss, sovereignty provides the state with the legal authority to control only that behavior occurring within its own territory.[3] Events and processes found beyond these territorial limits are more difficult to regulate, especially for underdeveloped states (see East, 1973:556–60). Vernon (1978–79:123–25) notes that this creates great difficulties for governments dealing with multinational corporations, because much of what the government may wish to regulate may be beyond its sovereign jurisdiction. For example, while the stock of investment and the profits that it generates are within the jurisdiction of the host state, decisions regarding flows and the expansion of operations may to a large extent occur beyond the state's sovereign reach. Governments therefore are constrained not only by their strength relative to the firm, but also are limited in that they only are able to pursue the portion of the overall corporate structure that is at hand.

It is within this context that one must consider the potential effects of foreign investment upon growth in underdeveloped countries. One might begin by addressing the arguments concerning flows of foreign investment. As was discussed above, there are strong reasons to doubt the market saturation arguments presented by Bornschier and Chase-Dunn (1985:81–82). While these specific arguments may be questionable, the basic premise behind them is sound: foreign investors should be expected to seek to regulate the flow of investments and the expansion of their operations according to the profits that they expect to reap from the commitment of resources to a host society. In addition, Bornschier and Chase-Dunn are accurate in implying that host states may find it difficult to regulate inflows of investments, because, as was just mentioned, such inflows occur largely as a result of decisions regarding multinational resource allocations that are made from beyond the host government's sovereign jurisdiction.

Thus, the key point of departure from Bornschier and Chase-Dunn in this analysis is not concerned with foreign investors' motivations but instead focuses upon the variable that will be the key factor for determining where foreign investors judge profit potential as highest. The basic argument here is that there will be a tendency to invest in markets that were previously regarded as valuable. Wealthier countries with high previous flows of investments meet this requirement. Wealth indicates the potential for ongoing markets and profits, and higher previous flows shows a degree of commitment that presumably reflects the judgment that the market is worthwhile.

Hence, the expectation is that future flows of foreign investment will be positively related to past flows in countries at a higher level of development, and there will be no relationship between stocks of foreign investment in (whatever sector) and flows.[4] This effect of past flows upon future flows should not be permanent and may be expected to diminish over time, as corporate strategies shift to adjust to new opportunities.

To the extent that a decision to expand operations is made, then growth should be encouraged, for such an expansion represents a greater employment of capital and more economic activity. As may be recalled from the discussion found above, increased capital use generally is regarded as a fundamental determinant of growth (see Papanek, 1973:121; Chenery and Syrquin, 1975:23). In particular, growth in modern sectors, such as manufacturing and transportation and communications, should be most affected. In manufacturing, the potential should be high for realizing the greater profits mentioned above, thus drawing more growth-producing capital to that sector.Growth in transportation and communications should be stimulated by the increased need to move and distribute goods that results from more economic activity.

While flows may be positively associated with growth, there is good reason to doubt that there will be the sort of positive association with increases in domestic investment that many analysts expect (see the above discussion of the liberal point of view). A consideration of the mechanisms by which expansions of corporate operations are financed serve as the source for these doubts. Reuber (1973:87–97), Barnet and Muller (1974:152–53), and I. Frank (1980:60–64) note that such expansion is funded from three sources: (1) inflows of capital from abroad, (2) borrowing from local credit markets, and (3) the reinvestments of the profits from local operations. To the extent that inflows are involved, then growth in domestic investment should be increased, for local capital availability becomes higher. Reinvestments of profits, which shall be considered below, should have a similar effect. Borrowing on local credit markets, however, may not increase domestic investment, for it may simply move capital from the hands of one potential investor (who may be local) to the hands of another investor (who is foreign).

Prior research by Reuber (1973:91) and Frank (1980:60–61) indicates that the tendency to resort to local borrowing is greatest when the expansion of local operations is largest, because foreign investors regard such borrowing as insulating them from some of the risks, such as access to foreign exchange to repay external debts, that are associated with operations abroad. Thus, as the degree of expansion becomes higher, the actual movement of capital from abroad remains relatively constant, and the proportion of local borrowing rises. It should be noted that the local government is in little position to force firms to maintain higher proportions of inflows for financing local expansion, because inflows occur as a result of activities that generally are beyond the host state's sovereign jurisdiction. Consequently, one should find no systematic relationship between measures of flows of foreign investment and growth in domestic investment unless one is able to separate out the specific amounts of those flows that represent local borrowing and inflows from abroad (which, as noted in note 4, cannot be done with current measures).[5]

As mentioned above, the reinvestment of the profits from local operations has the potential for increasing growth in local investment. The same is true for the foreign exchange payments from mining projects. Each of these activities occurs within the sovereign reach of the host government and therefore should be subject to regulation. The reinvestment of at least a portion of the profits from foreign activities, as opposed to the wholesale repatriation that some authors discuss (see the above arguments), is in the best interests of the host government and should be perceived by government officials as one means for pursuing the goal of economic growth. Since the government has the authority to require compliance and since it also controls legal access to the foreign exchange needed for repatriating profits, one might anticipate that the government would demand the reinvestment of profits in an effort to promote growth in domestic investment, hoping that this in turn would lead to higher growth.

A similar situation should be found regarding mining investments. As noted in Chapter 3, investments in this sector constitute an important source of foreign exchange for underdeveloped countries. At the same time, these investments are controversial, are regarded as exploitative, and are not perceived as providing the corporation with fundamental advantages in its relationship with the host government. Under these conditions, the host government is in a favorable position for using mining investments to further the pursuit of economic growth. This may be done by requiring foreign exchange payments that are used to further growth in domestic investment. Presumably, the size of foreign exchange payments will be highest when stocks of foreign investment in the mining sector are largest.

Thus, the expectation is that flows of foreign investment (as measured with currently available data) are not related to growth in domestic investment, while the total profits from foreign operations and the stocks of foreign investment in mining are positively related. The impact both of profits and of stocks in mining should be relatively immediate, because profits should be reinvested as they occur, and, as the results in Chapter 3 indicate, foreign exchange from mining operations is quickly available for use in the host state.

In the case both of the reinvestment of profits and of the greater foreign exchange availability resulting from larger stocks in mining, the impact upon growth in domestic investment should lead to indirect effects upon growth in the production found in the host economy, as domestic investment is used to promote economic growth. One might expect these indirect effects to concentrate in the manufacturing sector. There are two reasons for this. One is that, as Cardoso and Faletto (1979:xix), Caporaso (1980:615), and Rothgeb (1986b:140) note, foreign manufacturing enterprises are more likely to derive their profits from sales in the host markets than are firms involved in other sorts of business, such as mining.[6] As a result, the reinvestment of profits may be expected to center on this sector. Reinforcing this tendency is the second reason for expecting growth to concentrate in manufacturing. This is the inclination on the part of local governmental officials to associate development with industrialization (see Holsti, 1975:827); Rothstein, 1977:173; Rothgeb, 1986b:140). Such a perception should move these officials to direct local investment toward the manufacturing sector and to pressure foreign investors to reinvest their profits in a similar way. In each case, the result should be higher short-term growth that reflects the fairly immediate effects of reinvestments and stocks in mining on domestic investments.

An appraisal of the political relationship between the multinational corporation and the host state should also provide clues as to the direct effects of foreign investment on growth. One might begin by considering the situation in the manufacturing sector. This is the sector in which economic activity should be most highly valued by local leaders, as was just noted. The fundamentally important elements for growth in this sector are capital, technological development, and entrepreneurial talent. To the extent that foreign investments make these sorts of contributions, they have the *potential* for aiding growth in underdeveloped societies. As was discussed in previous chapters, these are precisely the sorts of inputs that host officials are likely to regard as coming from a multinational corporate presence, particularly when the investments are in manufacturing (see Vernon, 1971:56; 1977:10–11; Evans, 1979:203; Frieden, 1981:407–13; Rothgeb, 1986a:127).

Whether foreign investment actually leads directly to growth in manufacturing should depend on several factors: (1) the level of development of the host state, (2) the degree to which local support structures are available, (3) the ability of the foreign corporation to reap profits, and (4) the ability and desire of the host government to coerce the corporation into contributing to local growth. The level of development of the host state should determine the relative extent of the corporation's contribution to local resources. In very poor societies, where capital, technology, and entrepreneurial talent are relatively scarce, the possible addition to resources should be great. In wealthier societies, where these ingredients for growth are more commonplace, the corporate impact should be less. The second condition is important, because any foreign investment–induced growth will be ephemeral unless local infrastructure and other support facilities, such as a dependable banking system, exist to magnify and feed off of the foreign activities (see Reuber, 1973:37, 151–52; Richardson, 1978:36–38). The third factor relates to the willingness of foreign investors to make commitments and continue putting in additional resources, thereby adding to local production and expanding the local economy. To the extent that profits are available, the pursuit of corporate goals will contribute to growth. Finally, the fourth condition pertains to the host government's strength relative to that of the corporation, which should be a basic determinant of the government's ability to force the corporation to contribute to the realization of the government's goal of growth.

If one ponders these conditions carefully and reflects on their level of mutual reinforcement, then the specific direct effects of foreign investment upon growth should become evident. It is expected that the greatest impact of foreign investment upon growth should be found in states that are the poorest and most dependent, because that is where the relative addition to resources should be greatest. These are precisely the sorts of societies, however, that tend to lack support structures, that have little potential for an ongoing expansion of profits, and whose governments are least capable or willing to seek to force foreign investors to feed resources on a continuing basis into the government's pursuit of growth.

This is the case both for foreign investments in manufacturing and in mining. On the one hand, foreign investments in each sector should be associated with immediate growth in poorer and more dependent societies. Manufacturing investments should produce growth because the introduction of foreign factories will expand production in the manufacturing sector, and mining investments should lead to growth by providing access to the foreign exchange needed to acquire the foreign-made equipment and machinery required to set up industrial operations. On the other hand, deficiencies relating to the other three conditions should exert untoward effects over time. First, problems pertaining to the lack of a well-developed network of infrastructure in poorer countries may create the tendency for foreign projects to exist in a virtual vacuum, affecting the host society only minimally. In addition, the banking systems in poorer countries may be unable to provide the magnitude of financing required for the ongoing expansion of foreign concerns. Second, the poverty found in the host society should limit the profits from manufacturing enterprises and restrict the ability to promote growth through the reinvestments discussed above. When combined with the frailties of the local banking system, this represents a major obstacle to the ability and willingness of foreign investors to pursue the sorts of action needed to promote growth. Not only are profits uncertain, thus bringing into question the ability to attain the primary corporate goals, but the corporation also may be forced to assume greater risks if it chooses to expand, because it cannot rely on local financing (see the above arguments).

Finally, the ability of the host government to compel foreign investors to aid local growth may be limited. With manufacturing investments, the government faces several problems. The first relates to the government's perception of vulnerability to investors in this sector. As was noted in Chapter 2, manufacturing investments may be valued as fundamentally important to development and as involving very complex and not easily replaced contributions (see Vernon, 1977:10–11; Frieden, 1981:407–13). Hence, governments in very poor and dependent societies may be quite reluctant to pursue vigorous policies designed to compel manufacturing investors to adopt practices of the government's choice if the corporations indicate a resistance to such policies. Beyond this, the government faces two practical difficulties. The first is associated with the limited growth in profits that may be available in very poor societies. One cannot compel corporate reinvestments to contribute to growth if the necessary growth in the corporate profit structure is not there to support these ever greater reinvestments.[7] The limited sovereign reach of the host government poses the second practical difficulty, for the government is in no position to force the corporation to expand local operations through the increased inflows from abroad that must of necessity come from beyond the government's jurisdiction.

In the case of mining investments, somewhat different problems are found. Here the government's perceived vulnerability to the foreign presence should diminish rapidly over time (see Chapter 2), and the government should regard itself as in a suitable position to seek concessions from the corporation that may be used to promote growth. Moran (1974) provides a superb discussion of the difficulties faced by the government when it attempts to use such tactics. For one thing, world market conditions as opposed to governmental demands, tend to set the levels of returns the government may obtain from mining investments. Except in rare circumstances, it is impossible to obtain a continuing rapid expansion of production to provide ever increasing pools of foreign exchange to promote increases in growth. Moreover, the international marketing structures for the products from mining investments generally are beyond host government control, thus reducing the government's ability to acquire higher levels of foreign exchange as it sees fit. Consequently, the ability to force the corporation to contribute to meet the government's goals regarding growth is limited even in the case of mining investments, where host state vulnerability is low.[8]

Thus, it is hypothesized that stocks of foreign investment in the manufacturing sector and in the mining sector will be positively related to growth in manufacturing. This effect, however, should be short-lived, as the problems associated with the ongoing promotion of growth manifest themselves over time. It is expected that the ephemeral nature of this growth and the lack of local support structures (especially in banking) may prevent any sort of spillover effect in very poor and dependent societies, wherein increased economic activity in the manufacturing sector creates the basis for greater activity elsewhere, such as in the transportation and communications sector.

As far as the effects upon the agricultural sector are concerned, the expectation is that foreign investments in manufacturing and in mining should have only incidental effects. That is, there is little reason to believe that multinational firms would concern themselves with activities in this sector, for the agricultural sector should be seen as at best peripheral to the corporate goal of profit making. Indeed, the arguments found in each of the schools of thought discussed above take precisely this sort of view, treating foreign investment as affecting growth in agriculture only in an indirect manner.

A perusal of the arguments regarding the effects of foreign investments on the agricultural sector reveal two basic types of indirect effects. The first is associated with the supposed effect of foreign investments both on local resource availability and on the facility with which they may be used. As has been argued, there are good reasons to believe that foreign investment may contribute to both of these factors by leading, under certain circumstances, to greater output in manufacturing and in transportation and communications. Hence, a potential indirect effect of this sort on agriculture cannot be dismissed.

A second set of projected effects on agriculture have to do with the reallocation of local resources away from the agricultural sector. One such reallocation has to do with a shift in the labor force from the agricultural sector to other sectors. To the extent that such a shift occurs and is not accompanied by a corresponding increase in labor productivity, one might well expect a decline in agricultural output. The basic problem with the arguments found in the literature is that there is no reason to believe that a multinational corporate presence will create such a shift. While it is beyond the scope of the present research to explain social changes of this sort, one would expect that such labor movements would reflect fundamental social processes, such as a rapidly expanding economy or an increasing ease of travel in society, that would bear little relationship to the presence or absence of a foreign corporate presence, except in the most indirect way.

Another presumed reallocative effect has to do with the government's decision to emphasize more modern sectors, such as manufacturing, while ignoring the agricultural sector, thereby hurting output. Many in the literature describe foreign investors as creating the climate that leads host officials to pursue this strategy. A consideration of the results from Chapters 2 and 3, however, points to different conclusions. It was found that foreign investments did contribute to the host government's access to resources (under a very specific set of circumstances), but that there was little reason to believe that foreign investors affected decisions regarding *how* those resources were used. In other words, the specific goals that the host government pursues, and the means that it selects to meet those goals, are a product of the preference schedules of host government officials and are not dictated by (or even much influenced by) multinational corporations. Thus, while host government policy preferences may well affect the agricultural sector, there would seem to be little reason to expect foreign investments to affect agricultural output by way of an impact on governmental policy preferences.

SUMMARY

If the foregoing discussion is correct, then foreign investments may be expected to have a very complex set of effects upon growth in underdeveloped host states. One may begin by summarizing the expected results pertaining to flows of foreign investments. It is hypothesized that (1) future flows of foreign investments will be positively related over the short run to past flows in countries at a higher level of development, (2) higher flows of foreign investment will be directly related to higher growth in the manufacturing and in the transportation and communications sectors, and (3) flows of foreign investment are not related to growth in domestic investment.

The expectations concerning the effects of the profits from foreign corporate operations are that (1) higher profits are related early on to higher growth in domestic investment, and (2) higher profits are associated with higher growth in manufacturing by way of the prior effect on growth in domestic investment. Stocks of foreign investment in mining are expected in general to have a similar set of effects, being positively related over the short-run to growth in domestic investment and to growth in manufacturing via this impact on domestic investment.

Finally, it is hypothesized that stocks of foreign investment both in manufacturing and in mining will be positively associated over the short run with growth in manufacturing in very poor and dependent countries.

As was done in previous chapters, controls are included in the analysis for variables that theoretical considerations point to as important. Rothgeb (1986b:141) notes that the total resource base of the host state is one such variable. This is controlled for using the total population of the host state, as in the earlier analysis. Other variables that are introduced into the analysis include controls for growth in domestic investment and for expenditures by the central government. Controlling for domestic investment allows one to consider the impact of the degree to which local resources are channeled toward the promotion of increased economic activity. Jackman (1982:187), Bornschier and Chase-Dunn (1985: 92), and Rothgeb (1984b:1067); 1984–85:1; 1986b:141) recommend the consideration of this control. The inclusion of central government expenditures allows one to control for the degree to which the government seeks to play a leading role in moving resources to seek enhanced growth, which, as was discussed in Chapter 3, is one of the key roles played by governments in underdeveloped countries.

RESEARCH DESIGN AND MEASUREMENT OF VARIABLES

The cross-national research design employed in Chapters 2 and 3 is utilized to examine the relationship between foreign investment and economic growth in underdeveloped societies. The dependent variable is economic growth. As mentioned earlier in this chapter, growth has been examined extensively in previous studies of the effects of foreign investment upon Third World states. In these studies, growth has been measured in at least four ways: (1) as the average annual real growth in gross national product per capita (see McGowan and Smith, 1978; Bornschier, 1981; Jackman, 1982; Bornschier and Chase-Dunn, 1985), (2) as the average annual real growth in gross domestic product per capita (see Dolan and Tomlin, 1980), (3) as the average annual real growth in gross domestic product (see Mahler, 1980), and (4) as the ratio of gross national product per capital in one year and gross national product per capita in a subsequent year (see Bornschier et al., 1978).

The present study departs from past studies by examining the growth occurring in specific sectors of the host economy. With the exception of Rothgeb's (1984a, 1984–85) work, such measures of growth have not been used previously. The measures for sectoral growth were based upon the average yearly real increase in the total amount of a state's gross domestic product that was derived from the manufacturing, transportation and communications, and agricultural sectors during each of the time periods studied (1967–69, 1970–72, 1973–75, and 1976–78).[9] Examining these sectors allows one to attain greater precision in ascertaining the effects of foreign investment upon growth, for one is able to investigate more modern sectors, such as manufacturing and transportation and communications, and more traditional sectors, such as agriculture. In order to avoid the potential problems that often accompany the study of growth (see Jackman, 1980:605–6; Markus, 1979:45–47), percentage real increases in growth were used instead of figures for absolute growth. Jackman (1980:606) recommends the use of such figures as a means for addressing the problem. The data for percentage real growth were precalculated in the data sources used (see Appendix 2).

The independent variables in this chapter are stock of foreign investment, flows of foreign investment, and the profits derived from foreign investments. Stock of foreign investment in manufacturing and in mining and the interaction terms for stock, the level of development of the host country, and the proportion of investment from the single largest foreign national source were measured using the same data and practices as were employed in previous chapters. The sole adjustment in these measurement procedures is that in the present chapter, the combined total stock of foreign investment in manufacturing and in mining from *all* foreign national sources was used instead of the total stock from the single largest foreign national source. This substitution was made because the combined total stock figure conforms more closely to the arguments found in the literature.[10]

Flows of foreign investment were operationalized using the continuous growth formula discussed in Chapter 3. As was discussed previously, this measure of flows is based upon the change over time in the value of stocks of foreign investment. Since sectoral breakdowns of stocks only were available for one year (1967), the measure of flows was based upon changes in total investment. This measure was used as a surrogate for sectoral flows (see Dolan and Tomlin, 1980:55; Rothgeb, 1986b:144). Data for total stocks were available only for 1967, 1971, 1973, 1975, and 1978; hence, the measures of flows were calculated for 1967–71, 1971–73, 1973–75, and 1975–78. These time periods were used to approximate the values for flows during the time periods examined in this analysis.

Terms representing the interaction between a high (or low) level of development and flows of foreign investment were created using dummy variables for a high and for a low level of development. The same dummy variables for high and low development that were employed in Chapters 2 and 3 were used for that purpose here. Creating the interaction terms involved multiplying the measure of flows by each of these dummy variables, resulting in two variables representing the interaction between a low level of development and flow (Lo Devel × Flows) and a high level of development and flows (HiDevel × Flows).

The effects of the profits from foreign investments upon growth and upon domestic investment were investigated by using the average value between 1967 and 1969 of net direct investment income weighted by total GDP in 1967 as the measure for profits. As reported by the World Bank (1976:9), this variable includes the remitted and unremitted earnings from the direct investments of nonnationals in the host country, net the value of the profits that the host state's nationals earn from their direct investments in other states.

Rothgeb (1986b:143) notes that using net direct investment income as an indicator for the profits of foreign investors in the host country requires that one make a key assumption. This is that citizens of the host state have fairly negligible holdings abroad when compared with foreign holdings in their own state. If this assumption holds, then the net figures provided by the World Bank (1976) will predominantly reflect the total profits of foreigners in the host state. This assumption is reasonable because, although there has been growth in the number of Third World–based multinational corporations in recent years, the income from such operations is still quite small when compared with the income that foreigners derive from operations in Third World states. Moreover, the magnitudes of the figures for direct investment income from the World Bank indicate that for every state for which there are data, foreigners earn overwhelmingly greater profits from their Third World operations than Third World corporations earn from their operations. Hence, this assumption appears acceptable.

Two variables representing the interaction between profits, a high or low level of development, and the proportion of the total stock (from all sectors) of foreign investment from the single largest foreign national source were created using the procedures outlined above. These interaction variables were employed to test assertions that extremely dependent and dominated countries are severely affected by the uses foreign investors find for their profits (see the above discussion regarding repatriation).

Four other variables are included in the analysis in this chapter. They are total population, growth in domestic investment, governmental management, and the change in the size of the agricultural labor force. Total population and governmental management were measured with the same techniques as were employed in previous chapters. Growth in domestic investment was measured as the average annual percentage real growth in gross domestic fixed capital formation that occurred during each of the time periods investigated. As was the case for the sectoral growth measures used above, the data source used provided precalculated figures for growth in domestic investment.[11]

Change in the agricultural labor force was measured as the difference between the percentage of the total labor force engaged in agriculture at one point in time and the percentage that was employed in such pursuits at a subsequent point in time. The source for these data (World Bank, *World Tables*, 1983) provided figures only for 1965, 1970, 1975, and 1980. Thus, the difference between 1965 and 1970 was used to approximate the difference between 1967 and 1969; the difference between 1970 and 1975, to approximate both 1970–72 and 1973–75; and the difference between 1975 and 1980, to approximate 1976–78.

Standard multiple regression analysis again was used to assess the effects of the independent variables on the dependent variables. Problems pertaining to multicollinearity required the use of separate regression equations to examine the main effects of each of the foreign investment variables and of the interaction terms. Scatterplots of the bivariate relationships between the independent and dependent variables revealed no apparent nonlinear relationships.[12]

The regression equations used to investigate the direct effects of foreign investment on growth may be illustrated by considering the equations used to analyze stock of foreign investment in manufacturing and growth in manufacturing:

(1) $\text{Man} = a + b1\text{TotInvMan} + b2\text{Pop} + e$

(2) $\text{Man} = a + b1\text{LoDevel} \times \text{HiConcen} \times \text{TotInvMan} + b2\text{Pop} + e$

(3) $\text{Man} = a + b1\text{HiDevel} \times \text{HiConcen} \times \text{TotInvMan} + b2\text{Pop} + e$

The effects of manufacturing investment upon growth in agriculture (Ag) and in transportation and communications (TC) were determined by substituting these variables into the above equations in place of growth in manufacturing. The impact of flows, profits, and investments in mining were analyzed by substituting each of these variables and the relevant interaction terms into these equations in the place of the manufacturing investment variables above.

The indirect effects of foreign investment upon growth by way of an effect on domestic investment (DomInv) were analyzed using two sets of equations. The first examined the effect on domestic investment. Once again, manufacturing investments provide the sample equations:

(4) $DomInv = a + b1TotInvMan + b2Pop + e$

(5) $DomInv = a + b1LoDevel \times HiConcen \times TotInvMan + b2Pop + e$

(6) $DomInv = a + b1HiDevel \times HiConcen \times TotInvMan + b2Pop + e$

Following this, domestic investment was examined for its effect on growth:

(7) $Man = a + b1TotInvMan + b2Pop + b3DomInv + e$

(8) $Man = a + b1LoDevel \times HiConcen \times TotInvMan + b2Pop + b3DomInv + e$

(9) $Man = a + b1HiDevel \times HiConcen \times TotInvMan + b2Pop + b3DomInv + e$

Foreign investments in mining, flows, and profits and the proper interaction terms were substituted in these equations when necessary to examine the impacts of these variables. The other sectoral measures of growth also were placed in the equations when necessary.

The indirect effects on growth via a prior impact on future flow (FuFlow) of foreign investment were tested as follows:

(10) $FuFlow = a + b1TotInvMan + b2Pop + e$

(11) $FuFlow = a + b1LoDevel \times HiConcen \times TotInvMan + b2Pop + e$

(12) $FuFlow = a + b1HiDevel \times HiConcen \times TotInvMan + b2Pop + e$

The effects of growth while controlling for future flows were examined with the following equations:

(13) $Man = a + b1TotInvMan + b2Pop + b3FuFlow + e$

(14) $Man = a + b1LoDevel \times HiConcen \times TotInvMan + b2Pop + b3FuFlow + e$

(15) $Man = a + b1HiDevel \times HiConcen \times TotInvMan + b2Pop + b3FuFlow + e$

Analogous equations were used to determine how investments in mining and past flows (during 1967–71) affected future flows. Growth in agriculture and in transportation and communications were substituted for growth in manufacturing where appropriate.

The effects of total stocks (all sources) in manufacturing on governmental management were examined with these equations:

(16) GovMan $= a + b1$TotInvMan $+ b2$Pop $+ e$

(17) GovMan $= a + b1$LoDevel $\times$ HiConcen $\times$ TotInvMan $+ b2$Pop $+ e$

(18) GovMan $= a + b1$HiDevel $\times$ HiConcen $\times$ TotInvMan $+ b2$Pop $+ e$

The effects of foreign investment on growth with a control for governmental management were determined using these equations:

(19) Man $= a + b1$TotInvMan $+ b2$Pop $+ b3$GovMan $+ e$

(20) Man $= a + b1$LoDevel $\times$ HiConcen $\times$ TotInvMan $+ b2$Pop $+ b3$GovMan $+ e$

(21) Man $= a + b1$HiDevel $\times$ HiConcen $\times$ TotInvMan $+ b2$Pop $+ b3$GovMan $+ e$

Similar equations substituting stock of investment in mining for manufacturing investments, and growth in agriculture and in transportation and communications for manufacturing growth, were used where appropriate.

The effects of foreign investments on changes in the agricultural labor force involved using the following equations:

(22) AgLab $= a + b1$TotInvMan $+ b2$Pop $+ e$

(23) AgLab $= a + b1$LoDevel $\times$ HiConcen $\times$ TotInvMan $+ b2$Pop $+ e$

(24) AgLab $= a + b1$HiDevel $\times$ HiConcen $\times$ TotInvMan $+ b2$Pop $+ e$

The resulting effect on growth in agriculture was determined with these equations:

(25) Ag $= a + b1$TotInvMan $+ b2$Pop $+ b3$AgLab $+ e$

(26) Ag $= a + b1$LoDevel $\times$ HiConcen $\times$ TotInvMan $+ b2$Pop $+ b3$AgLab $+ e$

(27) Ag $= a + b1$HiDevel $\times$ HiConcen $\times$ TotInvMan $+ b2$Pop $+ b3$AgLab $+ e$

Obtaining the results for mining investments involved substituting in these equations for the relevant manufacturing investment variables.

Finally, the effects of growth in modern sectors on growth in agriculture involved using these equations:

(28) Ag $= a + b1$TotInvMan $+ b2$Pop $+ b3$Man $+ e$

(29) Ag $= a + b1$LoDevel $\times$ HiConcen $\times$ TotInvMan $+ b2$Pop $+ b3$ Man $+$
    e

(30) Ag $= a + b1$HiDevel $\times$ HiConcen $\times$ TotInvMan $+ b2$Pop $+ b3$ Man $+$
    e

The impact of growth in transportation and communications was determined by substituting for Man, and the effects of mining investments were analyzed by replacing the manufacturing investment variables with the proper mining variables.

The synchronic and time-lagged analysis utilized in Chapters 2 and 3 were employed again in the present chapter. In the synchronic analysis, all variables were measured for 1967–69. For the time-lagged analysis, the independent variables were measured for 1967–69, and the dependent and the control variables were measured for 1970–72, 1973–75, and 1976–78. As in Chapter 3, the assessment of the indirect effects of foreign investment involved measuring the foreign investment variables for 1967–69 and lagging the intervening variables to coincide with the measures for the dependent variables. There were two exceptions to these procedures. One occurred in the examination of the effects of past flows on future flows, where flows in 1967–71 were examined for their effects upon flows in 1971–73, 1973–75, and 1976–78. The second involved change in the agricultural labor force, where the dearth of available data meant that the time-lagged analysis of the effect of foreign investment on the agricultural labor force would pertain to 1965–70 (approximating the no-lagged effects), 1970–75 (approximating the three-year-lagged effects), and 1975–80 (approximating the nine-year-lagged effects). When the effect of change in the agricultural labor force on growth in agriculture was examined, the effect of the 1965–70 measure of the former variable on the 1967–69 measure of the latter variable was considered, the 1970–75 measure of the former was paired both with the 1970–72 and the 1973–75 measures of the latter, and the 1975–80 measure of the former was paired with the 1976–78 measure of the latter.

RESULTS

The analysis in this chapter begins by considering the direct effects upon growth of stocks of foreign investment in manufacturing and in mining, flows of foreign investment, and the profits earned by foreign investors. These results are in Tables 4.1 through 4.4. Table 4.1 reveals a short-term positive relationship between foreign investments in manufacturing and growth in manufacturing, followed by a negative relationship after three years, with these effects being centered in poor countries with a high concentration of investment from one source. This result conforms well with the refined theoretical expectations discussed above. Very poor and dependent countries seem to experience higher

Table 4.1
Foreign Investments in Manufacturing and Growth in Manufacturing, Transportation and Communications, and Agriculture

Dependent Variable	Time Lag	TotInvMan	LoDevel x HiConcen x TotInvMan	HiDevel x HiConcen x TotInvMan	Pop	R^2	N
	No Lag	.30*			.00	.06	62
			.36**		-.03	.11	62
				-.06	-.08	-.02	62
Growth in Man.	Three Year	-.33**			.14	.12	68
			-.33**		.18	.13	68
				-.07	.21	.02	68
	Six Year	.00			.16	.00	67
			.00		.16	.00	67
				.04	.17	.00	67
	Nine Year	.20			.04	.00	62
			.23		.02	.02	62
				-.10	-.02	-.02	62
	No Lag	-.04			-.01	-.03	64
			-.02		.00	-.03	64
				-.06	-.01	-.03	64
Growth in Trans. and Comm.	Three Year	-.14			.16	.03	68
			-.10		.19	.02	68
				-.04	.19	.01	68
	Six Year	-.03			.05	-.03	67
			-.05		.05	-.03	67
				-.03	.05	-.03	67
	Nine Year	.00			.03	-.03	63
			-.03		.03	-.03	63
				-.01	.03	-.03	63
	No Lag	.11			.20	.01	64
			.02		.17	.00	64
				.10	.18	.01	64
Growth in Agr.	Three Year	.17			.14	.01	68
			.04		.10	-.02	68
				-.01	.09	-.02	68
	Six Year	-.06			-.03	-.03	68
			.01		-.01	-.03	68
				-.13	-.04	-.01	68
	Nine Year	-.32*			.12	.11	63
			-.38**		.16	.15	63
				.11	.22	.02	63

*p<.05
**p<.01

Table 4.2
Foreign Investments in Mining and Growth in Manufacturing, Transportation and Communications, and Agriculture

Dependent Variable	Time Lag	TotInvMin	LoDevel x HiConcen x TotInvMin	HiDevel x HiConcen x TotInvMin	Pop	R^2	N
	No	-.10			-.09	-.02	57
	Lag		.23		-.06	.02	57
				.00	-.07	-.03	57
Growth in Man.	Three Year	.13			.28*	.04	61
			-.43***		.23*	.22	61
				.10	.26	.03	61
	Six Year	.30*			.24	.07	61
			-.09		.14	-.01	61
				.04	.15	-.01	61
	Nine Year	.09			.04	-.03	56
			.00		.02	-.04	56
				.02	.02	-.04	56
	No	-.09			-.05	-.03	57
	Lag		.03		-.02	-.03	57
				-.04	-.03	-.03	57
Growth in Trans. and Comm.	Three Year	.00			.21	.01	61
			-.05		.21	.01	61
				.09	.22	.02	61
	Six Year	-.05			.03	-.03	60
			-.03		.04	-.03	60
				-.01	.04	-.03	60
	Nine Year	-.06			.00	-.03	56
			-.02		.02	-.04	56
				-.01	.02	-.04	56
	No	.22			.29*	.06	58
	Lag		-.26*		.21	.08	58
				.27*	.27*	.08	58
Growth in Agr.	Three Year	.09			.08	-.02	61
			.24		.06	.03	61
				.08	.07	-.03	61
	Six Year	.05			.00	-.03	61
			-.06		-.02	-.03	61
				-.10	-.04	-.02	61
	Nine Year	.19			.30*	.06	56
			-.09		.24	.03	56
				.10	.26	.03	56

*p<.05
***p<.001

immediate growth due to the additional resources and productive capacity introduced by manufacturing investors. This higher growth is ephemeral, however, disappearing almost immediately as the effects of the lack of local support structures come into play and the formerly high rate of growth declines relative to the rates of growth found in other countries.[13]

Foreign manufacturing investments appear to have little effect on growth in

Table 4.3

Flows of Foreign Investments and Growth in Manufacturing, Transportation and Communications, and Agriculture

Dependent Variable	Time Lag	Flows	LoDevel x Flows	HiDevel x Flows	Pop	R²	N
	No	.23			-.10	.03	62
	Lag		.02		-.08	-.03	62
				.17	-.05	.00	62
Growth in Man.	Three Year	.26*			.19	.09	68
			.10		.19	.03	68
				.21	.25*	.06	68
	Six Year	.28*			.14	.08	67
			.19		.12	.03	67
				.03	.17	.00	67
	Nine Year	.19			-.02	.00	62
			.17		-.05	.00	62
				-.03	-.01	-.03	62
	No	.00			.00	-.03	64
	Lag		-.10		.02	-.02	64
				-.10	-.02	-.02	64
Growth in Trans. and Comm.	Three Year	.30*			.17	.10	68
			.09		.17	.02	68
				.13	.22	.03	68
	Six Year	.00			.06	-.03	67
			-.01		.06	-.03	67
				-.02	.05	-.03	67
	Nine Year	.01			.03	-.03	63
			.00		.03	-.03	63
				-.02	.03	-.03	63
	No	.07			.16	.00	64
	Lag		.03		.16	.00	64
				.28*	.21	.07	64
Growth in Agr.	Three Year	.23			.08	.03	68
			.11		.07	-.01	68
				.12	.12	-.01	68
	Six Year	-.07			.00	-.03	67
			-.03		.00	-.03	67
				-.18	-.04	.00	67
	Nine. Year	-.07			.21	.01	62
			-.10		.22	.02	62
				.00	.20	.01	62

*p<.05

transportation and communications. The only effect upon the agricultural sector is the negative relationship that appears after nine years and that is most prevalent among poor and dependent countries, implying that manufacturing investments may be associated with some form of agricultural neglect.

The initial findings for investments in mining are in Table 4.2. These results reveal a negative effect upon growth in manufacturing after three years among

Table 4.4

Foreign Investment Profits and Growth in Manufacturing, Transportation and Communications, and Agriculture

Dependent Variable	Time Lag	Profit	LoDevel x HiConcen x Profit	HiDevel x HiConcen x Profit	Pop	R^2	N
	No	-.10			.28	.04	49
	Lag		.10		.25	.04	49
				-.02	.26	.03	49
Growth in Man.	Three Year	-.13			.26	.04	52
			-.03		.24	.02	52
				.15	.22	.04	52
	Six Year	-.19			.30*	.08	51
			.03		.28	.04	51
				-.08	.29*	.05	51
	Nine Year	-.15			.08	-.02	46
			-.03		.06	-.04	46
				.15	.04	-.02	46
	No	.13			-.02	-.03	50
	Lag		.05		.00	-.04	50
				-.02	.00	-.04	50
Growth in Trans. and Comm.	Three Year	-.13			.16	.00	53
			-.22		.16	.03	53
				.07	.13	-.01	53
	Six Year	-.13			.08	-.02	51
			.02		.06	-.04	51
				.04	.05	-.04	51
	Nine Year	-.12			.07	-.03	45
			.03		.04	-.04	45
				.02	.04	-.05	45
	No	-.15			.22	.02	49
	Lag		.31*		.15	.09	49
				-.12	.21	.01	49
Growth in Agr.	Three Year	-.03			.07	-.04	52
			.00		.06	-.04	52
				.03	.06	-.04	52
	Six Year	-.02			-.04	-.04	51
			-.04		-.04	-.04	51
				.14	-.06	-.02	51
	Nine Year	-.35*			.18	.10	46
			-.15		.14	-.01	46
				-.17	.16	.00	46

*p<.05

poor and dependent societies and a positive relationship after six years for the sample as a whole. There was no relationship with growth in transportation and communications. In agriculture, there were opposite immediate effects, depending on whether one considered poorer or wealthier dependent countries. Among poorer dependent states, the effect was negative. Among wealthier states, it was positive. Comment upon these results, which do not conform to the theoretical expectations outlined above, shall await the consideration of the indirect effects.

Table 4.3 has the results for flows. Positive relationships are found for the total sample after three and six years between flows and growth in manufacturing. A positive association also is found after three years for growth in transportation and communications. In addition, wealthier dependent countries display an immediate positive association between growth in agriculture and flows. For the most part, these results conform to the expectations discussed above.

The analysis of the relationship between profits and growth is reported in Table 4.4. Profits have no direct relationship with growth either in manufacturing or in transportation and communications. In agriculture, higher profits are associated with less immediate growth in very poor and dependent countries. Among all states, high profits are associated with greater growth in agriculture after nine years.[14] These findings for agriculture indicate that while more profitable foreign operations in very poor and dependent countries are associated with processes that harm the agricultural sector early on, the overall tendency is for greater profits to provide the sort of increased resource availability that benefits the agricultural sector over time.

The next set of tables reports the results concerned with the effects of foreign investment upon growth when the level of domestic investment is considered. Tables 4.5 through 4.8 illustrate the relationships between foreign investment and domestic investment. Table 4.5 shows that there is no relationship between foreign manufacturing investments and domestic investment. Table 4.6 indicates that no immediate positive relationship exists between investments in mining and growth in domestic investment. In Table 4.7, one finds no association between flows and domestic investment, and in Table 4.8, higher profits from foreign investment are strongly related to a higher level of growth in domestic investment after three years. These findings conform closely to the expectations outlined above in the revised theoretical discussion.

Tables 4.9 through 4.12 illustrate the association between foreign investment and growth when there are controls for growth in domestic investment. In each case, the relationships between foreign investment and the sectoral measures of growth are substantially the same as the results that are reported in Tables 4.1 through 4.4, where there were no controls for domestic investment. The results for the effects of domestic investment reveal a relatively strong positive relationship after three years between domestic investment and growth in manufacturing, a relationship that continues for up to nine years. Except for a small positive effect upon growth on transportation and communications after three years when mining investments in poor and dependent countries are considered, growth in domestic investment is unrelated to growth in the other sectors considered. These findings indicate that the profits from foreign investment and mining investments, both of which are associated with higher growth in domestic investment, are indirectly related to higher growth in manufacturing by way of their prior effect on domestic investment. At the same time, the results also reinforce the argument outlined above that the priorities of the leadership in

Table 4.5
Foreign Investments in Manufacturing and Growth in Domestic Investments

Time Lag	TotInvMan	LoDevel x HiConcen x TotInvMan	HiDevel x HiConcen x TotInvMan	Pop	R^2	N
No	.04			.02	−.03	64
Lag		.00		.00	−.03	64
			−.14	−.02	−.01	64
Three	−.15			.03	.00	68
Year		.00		.06	−.03	68
			−.04	.06	−.02	68
Six	.02			.11	−.02	67
Year		.13		.12	.00	67
			−.07	.09	−.02	67
Nine	.12			.21	.01	61
Year		.13		.20	.02	61
			.14	.21	.02	61

underdeveloped societies are oriented toward promoting growth and development in the manufacturing sector.

The next set of findings pertains to the relationship between foreign investment and growth when future flows of foreign investment are considered. Tables 4.13 through 4.15 report the associations between stocks and past flows of foreign investment and future flows of foreign investment. In Table 4.13, one finds that stocks in manufacturing are unrelated to future flows. Table 4.14 shows that the same is true for stocks in mining. Table 4.15, however, indicates that higher past flows are associated for up to nine years with higher future flows and that the relationship is most prevalent in wealthier Third World states. The results support the theoretical expectations in the above discussion and cast strong doubt upon the arguments of those who regard flows as declining over time when stocks are high (see Bornschier et al., 1978; Bornschier, 1981; Bornschier and Chase-Dunn, 1985).

Controlling for flows of foreign investment as is done in Tables 4.16 and 4.17 has little effect upon the relationship between stock of foreign investment (in manufacturing or in mining) and growth in any of the three sectors considered. The results for the effects of flows upon growth are also similar to the findings obtained when stocks were not included in the equations with flows: flows are positively associated with growth in manufacturing and in transportation and communications after three years. Introducing stocks into the equation merely

Table 4.6

Foreign Investments in Mining and Growth in Domestic Investments

Time Lag	TotInvMin	LoDevel x HiConcen x TotInvMin	HiDevel x HiConcen x TotInvMin	Pop	R^2	N
No Lag	.35*			.13	.07	58
		-.02		.02	-.04	58
			.00	.02	-.04	58
Three Year	-.17			.03	.00	61
		.12		.08	-.01	61
			.03	.09	-.03	61
Six Year	-.03			.07	-.03	61
		.23		.08	.03	61
			-.02	.08	-.03	61
Nine Year	.16			.24	.03	55
		.04		.20	.01	55
			.05	.22	.01	55

*$p < .05$

Table 4.7

Flow of Foreign Investments and Growth in Domestic Investments

Time Lag	Flows	LoDevel x Flow	HiDevel x Flow	Pop	R^2	N
No Lag	.13			.00	-.02	64
		.06		.00	-.03	64
			.10	.02	-.02	64
Three Year	.03			.06	-.03	68
		.13		.03	-.01	68
			.15	.09	.00	68
Six Year	.02			.10	-.02	67
		.06		.09	-.02	67
			-.09	.09	-.01	67
Nine Year	.05			.18	.00	61
		-.07		.20	.00	61
			-.04	.17	.00	61

makes it uncertain as to whether the positive relationship for growth in manufacturing extends further into the future, as was the case when stocks were not included.

The next set of tables relates to the association between foreign investment and growth when the role of governmental participation is considered. Tables 4.18 and 4.19 report the relationships between stock of foreign investment in manufacturing and in mining and governmental management. The results parallel

Table 4.8
Foreign Investment Profits and Growth in Domestic Investments

Time Lag	Profit	LoDevel x HiConcen x Profit	HiDevel x HiConcen x Profit	Pop	R^2	N
No	-.06			.04	-.04	50
Lag		-.23		.05	.01	50
			.12	.00	-.03	50
Three	-.49***			.13	.21	53
Year		.05		.06	-.03	53
			.05	.06	-.03	53
Six	-.06			.22	.01	51
Year		.18		.20	.04	51
			.04	.21	.01	51
Nine	.05			.06	-.04	46
Year		-.28		.09	.04	46
			-.24	.11	.02	46

***p<.001

the findings in Chapter 3.[15] Total stock of foreign investment in manufacturing is positively associated in Table 4.18 with governmental management after nine years, with the relationship centering on very poor and dependent societies. Stocks of investment in mining are not related to governmental management (Table 4.19).

Including governmental management in the regression analysis pertaining to growth produces some interesting results. In Table 4.20 the relationships between foreign manufacturing investments and growth in manufacturing and in transportation and communications are unaffected by the inclusion of governmental management. The results for growth in agriculture are a different story. The negative relationship after nine years evaporates with the introduction of a control for the role of the government, indicating that it is governmental priorities that are responsible for lower agricultural growth instead of foreign manufacturing investments. There is a moderately strong negative relationship between management and growth in agriculture after nine years.

Table 4.21 also reveals a substantial impact for governmental management upon the relationship between foreign investments in mining and growth in manufacturing. The pattern that emerges for very poor countries with a high concentration of investment from one foreign national source is similar to the pattern found when foreign manufacturing investments are examined: there is an immediate positive relationship followed by a negative relationship after three years. At the same time, the positive relationship after six years found in Table 4.1 disappears, indicating that it was spurious. This pattern matches closely the expectations in the theoretical discussion outlined above.

In the agricultural sector, including governmental management in the analysis produces an immediate positive relationship between stocks in mining and growth in agriculture in wealthier dependent countries and leads to a decline in the level

Table 4.9

Foreign Investments in Manufacturing and Growth in Manufacturing, Transportation and Communications, and Agriculture, Controlling for Domestic Investments

Dependent Variable	Time Lag	TotInvMan	LoDevel x HiConcen x TotInvMan	HiDevel x HiConcen x TotInvMan	Pop	DomInv	R^2	N
	No	.30*			.00	.02	.04	62
	Lag		.36**		-.03	.00	.09	62
				-.06	-.09	.02	-.04	62
Growth in Man.	Three Year	-.28*			.13	.31**	.21	68
			-.33**		.16	.34**	.24	68
				-.05	.19	.34**	.13	68
	Six Year	.00			.13	.32**	.09	67
			-.05		.12	.33**	.09	67
				.06	.14	.32**	.09	67
	Nine Year	.18			.02	.09	-.01	61
			.22		.00	.08	.01	61
				-.12	-.06	.13	-.02	61
	No	-.04			-.01	.05	-.05	64
	Lag		-.02		.00	.04	-.05	64
				-.05	-.01	.03	-.05	64
Growth in Trans. and Comm.	Three Year	-.11			.16	.20	.05	68
			-.12		.17	.23	.06	68
				-.03	.18	.21	.04	68
	Six Year	-.03			.05	-.01	-.04	66
			-.05		.05	.00	-.04	66
				-.04	.05	-.01	-.04	66
	Nine Year	.00			.02	.03	-.05	60
			-.05		.02	.04	-.05	60
				-.02	.02	.03	-.05	60
	No	.11			.19	.01	-.01	64
	Lag		.02		.17	.02	-.02	64
				.10	.18	.03	-.01	64
Growth in Agr.	Three Year	.20			.13	.20	.03	68
			.04		.09	.17	-.01	68
				.00	.08	.17	-.01	68
	Six Year	-.06			-.03	.00	-.04	67
			.01		-.01	.00	-.05	67
				-.13	-.04	.00	-.03	67
	Nine Year	-.32*			.12	.06	.10	61
			-.38**		.15	.08	.14	61
				.11	.23	.00	.01	61

*$p < .05$
**$p < .01$

of significance in the immediate negative relationship between these two variables among poorer dependent countries. In the case of the latter relationship, however, the magnitude of the beta coefficient changes very little, indicating that a weak relationship remains.

As far as the effects of governmental management upon growth are concerned, the negative relationship with agricultural growth after nine years that was present

Table 4.10
Foreign Investments in Mining and Growth in Manufacturing, Transportation and Communications, and Agriculture, with a Control for Domestic Investment

Dependent Variable	Time Lag	TotInvMin	LoDevel x HiConcen x TotInvMin	HiDevel x HiConcen x TotInvMin	Pop	DomInv	R^2	N
	No	-.11			-.10	.07	-.04	57
	Lag		.23		-.07	.06	.01	57
				.00	-.07	.06	-.05	57
Growth in Man.	Three Year	.20			.27*	.38**	.17	61
			-.48****		.20	.40***	.37	61
				.09	.23	.34**	.14	61
	Six Year	.31*			.21	.33**	.17	61
			-.17		.11	.36**	.10	61
				.04	.12	.32*	.08	61
	Nine Year	.11			.02	.11	-.03	55
			.00		-.01	.13	-.04	55
				.01	-.01	.13	-.04	55
	No	-.12			-.06	.09	-.04	57
	Lag		.03		-.02	.06	-.05	57
				-.04	-.03	.05	-.05	57
Growth in Trans. and Comm.	Three Year	.05			.20	.25	.06	61
			-.08		.19	.26*	.06	61
				.09	.20	.24	.06	61
	Six Year	-.05			.03	-.02	-.05	60
			-.03		.04	.00	-.05	60
				-.01	.04	-.02	-.05	60
	Nine Year	-.07			.00	.04	-.05	54
			-.02		.02	.03	-.06	54
				-.02	.01	.03	-.06	54
	No	.23			.29*	-.03	.04	58
	Lag		-.25		.21	.04	.06	58
				.27*	.27*	.04	.07	58
Growth in Agr.	Three Year	.13			.08	.25	.02	61
			.22		.04	.21	.06	61
				.07	.05	.23	.01	61
	Six Year	.05			-.01	.03	-.05	61
			-.07		-.03	.04	-.05	61
				-.10	-.05	.02	-.04	61
	Nine Year	.16			.30*	-.02	.03	55
			-.09		.25	.01	.02	55
				.11	.27	.00	.02	55

*p<.05
**p<.01
***p<.001
****p<.0001

in Table 4.20 in the results for manufacturing is also found when mining investments are examined in Table 4.21. In addition, governmental management is associated positively after nine years with growth in manufacturing when foreign investments in both manufacturing and mining are considered. The only

Table 4.11

Flows of Foreign Investments and Growth in Manufacturing, Transportation and Communications, and Agriculture, Controlling for Domestic Investments

Dependent Variable	Time Lag	Flows	LoDevel x Flows	HiDevel x Flows	Pop	DomInv	R^2	N
	No	.23			-.10	.02	.01	62
	Lag		.02		-.08	.02	-.04	62
				.17	-.05	.00	-.02	62
Growth in Man.	Three Year	.25*			.17	.34**	.19	68
			.05		.18	.34**	.13	68
				.16	.22	.32**	.15	68
	Six Year	.28*			.11	.31**	.17	67
			.17		.09	.31*	.11	67
				.06	.14	.33**	.09	67
	Nine Year	.18			-.05	.10	-.01	61
			.18		-.08	.13	-.01	61
				-.03	-.04	.11	-.04	61
	No	.00			.00	.04	-.04	64
	Lag		-.10		.03	.05	-.04	64
				-.10	-.02	.05	-.04	64
Growth in Trans. and Comm.	Three Year	.29*			.16	.20	.13	68
			.06		.17	.21	.05	68
				.10	.20	.20	.05	68
	Six Year	.00			.05	-.01	-.05	66
			-.01		.05	.00	-.05	66
				-.02	.05	-.01	-.05	66
	Nine Year	.00			.02	.02	-.05	60
			.00		.02	.02	-.05	60
				-.02	.02	.02	-.05	60
	No	.07			.16	.00	-.02	64
	Lag		.03		.16	.02	-.02	64
				.28*	.21	.00	.06	64
Growth in Agr.	Three Year	.22			.07	.16	.04	68
			.09		.06	.16	.00	68
				.10	.10	.15	.00	68
	Six Year	-.07			.00	.00	-.04	67
			-.03		.00	.00	-.05	67
				-.18	-.04	-.01	-.02	67
	Nine Year	-.08			.21	.03	.00	61
			-.10		.23	.02	.00	61
				.00	.20	.02	-.01	61

*p<.05
**p<.01

exception to this is when manufacturing stocks in poor and dependent societies are considered, and even here the magnitude of the beta coefficient is sufficiently close to that found in other equations to show evidence of a weak positive relationship. For the most part, these results reinforce the findings for domestic investment and lend additional credence to the arguments of theorists who suggest that the domestic political leadership in underdeveloped countries prefers

Table 4.12

Foreign Investment Profits and Growth in Manufacturing, Transportation and Communications, and Agriculture, Controlling for Domestic Investments

Dependent Variable	Time Lag	Profit	LoDevel x HiConcen x Profit	HiDevel x HiConcen x Profit	Pop	DomInv	R²	N
	No	-.09			.27	.19	.05	49
	Lag		.15		.23	.23	.07	49
				-.05	.26	.20	.05	49
Growth	Three	.13			.19	.55***	.26	52
in	Year		-.05		.22	.49***	.25	52
Man.				.12	.19	.48***	.26	52
	Six	-.17			.23	.32*	.16	51
	Year		-.03		.20	.34*	.13	51
				-.09	.22	.33*	.14	51
	Nine	-.17			.06	.40**	.13	46
	Year		.09		.03	.42**	.11	46
				.26	-.01	.45**	.16	46
	No	.13			-.02	-.02	-.05	50
	Lag		.04		.00	-.02	-.06	50
				-.01	.00	-.03	-.06	50
Growth in	Three	-.09			.14	.09	-.02	53
Trans.	Year		-.22		.15	.14	.03	53
and Comm.				.07	.12	.13	-.02	53
	Six	-.13			.09	-.05	-.04	51
	Year		.03		.07	-.05	-.06	51
				.04	.06	-.04	-.06	51
	Nine	-.14			.06	.08	-.05	45
	Year		.05		.03	.08	-.06	45
				.04	.03	.08	-.07	45
	No	-.15			.22	-.02	.00	49
	Lag		.32*		.15	.06	.08	49
				-.12	.21	.00	-.01	49
Growth	Three	.07			.04	.21	-.02	52
in	Year		-.01		.05	.18	-.02	52
Agr.				.02	.05	.18	-.02	52
	Six	-.03			.01	-.23	-.01	51
	Year		.00		.00	-.23	-.01	51
				.15	-.01	-.23	.01	51
	Nine	-.35*			.17	.04	.08	46
	Year		-.16		.14	-.02	-.03	46
				-.17	.15	-.01	-.02	46

*p<.05
**p<.01
***p<.001

in general to direct resources toward growth in manufacturing at the expense of the agricultural sector.

Tables 4.22 and 4.23 report the results for the association between foreign investment and growth in agriculture when the change in the agricultural labor force is considered. These tables illustrate that neither foreign investments in

Table 4.13

Foreign Investments in Manufacturing and Future Flows of Foreign Investments

Time Lag	TotInvMan	LoDevel x HiConcen x TotInvMan	HiDevel x HiConcen x TotInvMan	Pop	R^2	N
No Lag	.05			.09	-.02	64
		.00		.09	-.03	64
			.05	.09	-.02	64
Three Year	.04			.07	-.03	68
		.01		.06	-.03	68
			-.02	.05	-.03	68
Six Year	.05			.17	.00	67
		.05		.17	.00	67
			.03	.17	.00	67
Nine Year	-.01			.01	-.03	62
		.07		.02	-.03	62
			-.06	.00	-.03	62

Table 4.14

Foreign Investments in Mining and Future Flows of Foreign Investments

Time Lag	TotInvMin	LoDevel x HiConcen x TotInvMin	HiDevel x HiConcen x TotInvMin	Pop	R^2	N
No Lag	.18			.14	.00	58
		.09		.08	-.02	58
			.00	.08	-.03	58
Three Year	.17			.15	.00	61
		.08		.10	-.02	61
			.06	.11	-.02	61
Six Year	.18			.21	.02	61
		.11		.16	.00	61
			.00	.16	-.01	61
Nine Year	-.04			.03	-.03	56
		.09		.04	-.03	56
			.00	.04	-.04	56

manufacturing nor foreign investments in mining have any effect upon changes in the agricultural labor force. No such impact was expected. The results also reveal that controls for changes in the agricultural labor force have no effect upon the relationship between stocks of foreign investment (in manufacturing or in mining) and growth in agriculture. Interestingly, change in the agricultural labor force exerts its strongest effect upon agricultural growth in the six-year-lagged results, where a negative relationship is found, indicating that declines in the size of the labor force are associated with greater growth. This suggests that investing in the mechanization of the agricultural sector *may* be an important component in improving output.

Table 4.15
Past Flows of Foreign Investments and Future Flows of Foreign Investments

Time Lag	Flows	LoDevel x Flows	HiDevel x Flows	Pop	R^2	N
Three	.41***			.02	.15	68
Year		.18		.01	.00	68
			.33**	.11	.08	68
Six	.13			.15	.01	67
Year		.04		.15	.00	67
			.28*	.20	.07	67
Nine	-.03			.01	-.03	62
Year		.06		.00	-.03	62
			-.09	.00	-.02	62

*p<.05
**p<.01
***p<.001

The final set of results examines the impact of foreign manufacturing and mining investments on growth in agriculture when growth in manufacturing and in transportation and communications are controlled for. Table 4.24 shows that controls for growth in manufacturing have little impact upon the effect of manufacturing investments on agricultural growth. The control for growth in transportation and communications, however, does have an impact, with the negative relationships found after nine years (see Table 4.1) disappearing with the introduction of a control. In its place, one finds a small, positive relationship after three years. These effects are very similar to those found in Table 4.20, where a control for governmental management was included in the analysis, implying strongly that the apparent detrimental effects of stocks in manufacturing on growth in agriculture are spurious.

Table 4.25 illustrates the relationships between mining investments and growth in agriculture when the growth occurring in other sectors is controlled for. The three-year-lagged findings indicate that growth in each of the other sectors has a masking effect upon the relationship between mining investments and agricultural growth when poor and dependent countries are considered. Controlling for manufacturing growth reveals a moderately strong positive relationship, and controlling for growth in transportation and communications reveals a small positive relationship among this subset of countries. In effect, when one controls for the negative impact of mining investments on growth in manufacturing and for the lack of any effect on growth in transportation and communications, both of which are positively related to agricultural growth in very poor and dependent countries, one finds that mining investments are useful for promoting greater agricultural output.

A consideration of the effects of growth in other sectors upon growth in agriculture reveals a consistent positive relationship after three years between growth in the transportation and communications sector and growth in the agricultural sector, implying that an improved distribution system is fundamental to greater agricultural output. The effects of growth in manufacturing tend to be

Table 4.16

Investments in Manufacturing and Growth in Manufacturing, Transportation and Communications, and Agriculture, Controlling for Flows

Dependent Variable	Time Lag	TotInvMan	LoDevel x HiConcen x TotInvMan	HiDevel x HiConcen x TotInvMan	Pop	Flows	R^2	N
	No	.29*			-.03	.22	.09	62
	Lag		.36**		-.05	.23	.15	62
				-.07	-.12	.24	.02	62
Growth in Man.	Three Year	-.35**			.11	.38***	.26	68
			-.33**		.16	.37***	.26	68
				-.06	.19	.37**	.15	68
	Six Year	.00			.13	.18	.01	67
			-.02		.13	.18	.01	67
				.03	.13	.18	.02	67
	Nine Year	.20			.04	.10	.00	62
			.23		.02	.08	.01	62
				-.10	-.03	.09	-.03	62
	No	-.04			-.02	.00	-.05	64
	Lag		-.02		.00	.00	-.05	64
				-.06	-.01	.00	-.05	64
Growth in Trans. and Comm.	Three Year	-.15			.13	.38**	.16	68
			-.10		.17	.37**	.15	68
				-.03	.17	.37**	.14	68
	Six Year	-.04			.03	.14	-.02	67
			-.06		.03	.14	-.02	67
				-.04	.03	.14	-.02	67
	Nine Year	.00			.03	-.02	-.05	63
			-.03		.03	-.01	-.05	63
				-.01	.03	-.02	-.05	63
	No	.11			.19	.07	.00	64
	Lag		.02		.16	.07	-.02	64
				.09	.18	.07	-.01	64
Growth in Agr.	Three Year	.17			.13	.08	.00	68
			.04		.10	.09	-.03	68
				-.01	.09	.09	-.03	68
	Six Year	-.06			-.02	-.06	-.04	67
			.02		.00	-.06	-.04	67
				-.13	-.03	-.05	-.03	67
	Nine Year	-.32*			.13	-.11	.10	62
			-.37**		.16	-.08	.14	62
				.10	.22	-.10	.01	62

*p<.05
**p<.01
***p<.001

most pronounced when one considers poorer and more dependent countries. As mentioned above, manufacturing growth is positively associated with agricultural growth after three years when mining investments are considered (see Table 4.25). There also is a longer-term positive relationship after nine years when manufacturing investments are examined. This suggests that while poor and

Table 4.17

Investments in Mining and Growth in Manufacturing, Transportation and Communications, and Agriculture, Controlling for Flows

Dependent Variable	Time Lag	TotInvMin	LoDevel x HiConcen x TotInvMin	HiDevel x HiConcen x TotInvMin	Pop	Flows	R^2	N
	No	-.12			-.13	.23	.01	57
	Lag		.21		-.08	.20	.05	57
				.00	-.09	.23	.00	57
Growth in Man.	Three Year	.07			.22	.36**	.15	61
			-.47****		.19	.41***	.38	61
				.08	.21	.36**	.15	61
	Six Year	.28*			.21	.14	.07	61
			-.11		.11	.20	.02	61
				.03	.12	.18	.00	61
	Nine Year	.09			.05	-.01	-.05	56
			.00		.02	-.01	-.06	56
				.02	.02	-.01	-.06	56
	No	-.09			-.06	.02	-.05	57
	Lag		.03		-.02	.00	-.06	57
				-.04	-.03	.00	-.05	57
Growth in Trans. and Comm.	Three Year	-.06			.15	.37**	.13	61
			-.08		.17	.36**	.13	61
				.07	.18	.35**	.13	61
	Six Year	-.08			.00	.16	-.02	60
			-.05		.02	.15	-.03	60
				-.01	.02	.15	-.03	60
	Nine Year	-.06			.00	-.02	-.05	56
			-.01		.02	-.01	-.06	56
				-.01	.02	-.02	-.06	56
	No	.23			.30*	-.06	.04	58
	Lag		-.26		.21	.00	.06	58
				.27*	.27*	-.02	.06	58
Growth in Agr.	Three Year	.07			.07	.11	-.03	61
			.24		.05	.10	.02	61
				.07	.06	.12	-.03	61
	Six Year	.06			.00	-.06	-.05	61
			-.06		-.02	-.04	-.05	61
				-.10	-.04	-.05	-.04	61
	Nine Year	.18			.30*	-.16	.07	56
			-.08		.25	-.16	.04	56
				.11	.27	-.17	.05	56

*p<.05
**p<.01
***p<.001
****p<.0001

more dependent countries may be inclined toward promoting the manufacturing sector at the expense of agriculture (as the results for governmental management and domestic investment suggest), there may be some spillover whereby improvements in the manufacturing sector lead to improvements in agriculture.

Table 4.18

Foreign Investments in Manufacturing and Governmental Management

Time Lag	TotInvMan	LoDevel x HiConcen x TotInvMan	HiDevel x HiConcen x TotInvMan	Pop	R^2	N
No Lag	-.07			-.17	-.01	55
		-.10		-.16	-.01	55
			.09	-.13	-.01	55
Three Year	.07			.00	-.03	65
		.05		-.01	-.03	65
			.10	.00	-.02	65
Six Year	.20			-.07	.02	65
		.24		-.08	.04	65
			-.07	-.13	-.01	65
Nine Year	.33**			-.04	.09	65
		.37**		-.07	.12	65
			-.06	-.12	-.02	65

**p<.01

Table 4.19

Foreign Investments in Mining and Total Governmental Management

Time Lag	TotInvMin	LoDevel x HiConcen x TotInvMin	HiDevel x HiConcen x TotInvMin	Pop	R^2	N
No Lag	-.19			-.23	.02	53
		-.19		-.17	.02	53
			-.10	-.18	.00	53
Three Year	-.08			-.07	-.03	59
		-.09		-.05	-.03	59
			-.03	-.05	-.03	59
Six Year	-.14			-.20	.01	59
		-.05		-.16	-.01	59
			-.05	-.17	-.01	59
Nine Year	-.10			-.20	.00	59
		-.08		-.17	.00	59
			-.10	-.19	.00	59

CONCLUSIONS

The empirical results in this chapter provide support for the theoretical arguments above that are built around the assumption that multinational corporations and underdeveloped host governments pursue their own specific interests and seek to use one another to this end wherever possible. The specific hypothesized relationships that are derived from these arguments generally were sustained by the analysis. For example, it was expected that future flows of foreign investment would be more affected by the amount of past flows and by the level of development of the host society than by the total stock of foreign investment. It also was expected that flows of foreign investment would have little effect

Table 4.20
Investments in Manufacturing and Growth in Manufacturing, Transportation and Communications, and Agriculture, Controlling for Governmental Management

Dependent Variable	Time Lag	TotInvMan	LoDevel x HiConcen x TotInvMan	HiDevel x HiConcen x TotInvMan	Pop	GovMan	R^2	N
	No	.46**			.17	.07	.15	50
	Lag		.48***		.10	.10	.18	50
				−.03	.03	.08	−.06	50
Growth in Man.	Three Year	−.35**			.09	.14	.12	64
			−.37**		.14	.14	.14	64
				−.09	.16	.13	.00	64
	Six Year	.02			.18	−.09	−.01	64
			.02		.18	−.09	−.01	64
				.04	.18	−.08	−.01	64
	Nine Year	.06			.08	.28*	.05	60
			.14		.08	.24	.06	60
				−.08	.05	.30*	.05	60
	No	−.02			.00	.01	−.06	52
	Lag		−.01		.00	.01	−.06	52
				−.08	−.01	.02	−.06	52
Growth in Trans. and Comm.	Three Year	−.13			.13	.07	.00	65
			−.12		.15	.07	.00	65
				−.06	.15	.07	−.01	65
	Six Year	−.02			.05	.03	−.05	64
			−.06		.05	.03	−.04	64
				−.04	.04	.03	−.05	64
	Nine Year	.00			.03	.05	−.05	61
			−.03		.03	.04	−.05	61
				−.01	.03	.04	−.05	61
	No	−.18			.07	.16	.01	51
	Lag		−.24		.09	.15	.04	51
				.09	.14	.15	−.01	51
Growth in Agr.	Three Year	.24			.14	.11	.03	64
			.07		.08	.13	−.02	64
				−.03	.07	.13	−.03	64
	Six Year	−.03			−.06	−.14	−.03	64
			.04		−.06	−.16	−.02	64
				−.16	−.09	−.16	.00	64
	Nine Year	−.22			.10	−.35**	.22	60
			−.22		.12	−.34*	.22	60
				.09	.15	−.44***	.19	60

*p<.05
**p<.01
***p<.001

upon growth in domestic investment but would have a relatively immediate positive association with growth in more modern sectors, such as manufacturing and transportation and communications. Each of these expectations was supported by the empirical results. The past flow of foreign investment in wealthier countries was positively associated with future flows, while stocks of foreign

Table 4.21

Investments in Mining and Growth in Manufacturing, Transportation and Communications, and Agriculture, with a Control for Governmental Management

Dependent Variable	Time Lag	TotInvMin	LoDevel x HiConcen x TotInvMin	HiDevel x HiConcen x TotInvMin	Pop	GovMan	R^2	N
	No	.00			.04	.08	-.06	49
	Lag		.43**		.07	.16	.18	49
				.07	.06	.08	-.05	49
Growth in Man.	Three Year	.17			.24	.15	.03	58
			-.52****		.13	.09	.28	58
				.10	.21	.14	.01	58
	Six Year	.15			.20	-.09	.01	59
			-.09		.15	-.12	.00	59
				.04	.16	-.11	-.01	59
	Nine Year	.17			.17	.38**	.11	55
			.03		.11	.36**	.08	55
				.07	.13	.37**	.08	55
	No	-.14			-.07	-.03	-.05	50
	Lag		.02		-.02	.00	-.06	50
				-.06	-.03	-.01	-.06	50
Growth in Trans. and Comm.	Three Year	.10			.20	.02	-.02	59
			-.08		.16	.00	-.02	59
				.09	.19	.02	-.02	59
	Six Year	-.04			.03	.02	-.05	58
			-.03		.04	.02	-.05	58
				-.01	.04	.02	-.05	58
	Nine Year	-.06			.01	.04	-.05	55
			-.01		.03	.04	-.06	55
				.00	.03	.04	-.06	55
	No	.37*			.30	.23	.11	49
	Lag		-.27		.14	.13	.06	49
				.32*	.23	.20	.09	49
Growth in Agr.	Three Year	.14			.07	.04	-.03	58
			.24		.06	.05	.01	58
				.07	.04	.03	-.05	58
	Six Year	.08			-.04	-.15	-.02	59
			-.07		-.07	-.16	-.02	59
				-.12	-.09	-.16	-.01	59
	Nine Year	.15			.21	-.40**	.20	55
			-.12		.16	-.43**	.19	55
				.07	.18	-.41**	.18	55

*p<.05
**p<.01
****p<.0001

investment (in either manufacturing or in mining) were not related. Higher flows were associated with higher growth in the manufacturing and transportation and communications sectors (although the growth was not immediate but began only after a short time), and the results reinforce arguments that the expansion of

Table 4.22

Foreign Investments in Manufacturing, Change in the Agricultural Labor Force, and Growth in Agriculture

Dependent Variable	Time Lag	TotInvMan	LoDevel x HiConcen x TotInvMan	HiDevel x HiConcen x TotInvMan	Pop	AgLab	R^2	N
	No	.15			-.06		.00	64
	Lag		.09		-.09		-.01	64
				.08	-.08		-.02	64
AgLab	Three	.20			.07		.01	68
	Year		.20		.04		.01	68
				-.22	-.02		.02	68
	Six	.21			.05		.01	67
	Year		.20		.02		.01	67
				-.22	-.03		.02	67
	Nine	.20			-.09		.02	60
	Year		.18		-.12		.02	60
				-.19	-.18		.02	60
	No	.11			.20	.00	-.01	64
	Lag		.02		.17	.02	-.02	64
				.10	.18	.01	-.01	64
Growth in Agr.	Three	.13			.13	.17	.02	68
	Year		.00		.09	.19	.00	68
				.03	.10	.21	.01	68
	Six	.02			.00	-.40**	.12	67
	Year		.09		.00	-.42***	.13	67
				-.23	-.05	-.45***	.17	67
	Nine	-.33*			.09	-.04	.10	60
	Year		-.38**		.14	-.03	.14	60
				.09	.19	-.08	.00	60

*p<.05
**p<.01
***p<.001

local operations by foreign investors is indeed closely tied to the use of local funds and credit.

The profits that foreign corporations derive from their operations in host underdeveloped countries and the foreign exchange obtained from foreign mining operations were both hypothesized as contributing to higher growth in domestic investment and through this relationship were expected to assist growth in the manufacturing sector. The results supported these hypotheses, indicating that host countries use their sovereign authority where possible to require foreign investors to pursue policies that help the host government to meet its goal of promoting development.

The results for foreign manufacturing investments illustrate the limits of the host state's ability to pressure multinational corporations, especially when the host society is poor and very dependent. It was hypothesized that the effects of manufacturing investments would be greatest in the manufacturing sector in poor

Table 4.23
Foreign Investments in Mining, Change in the Agricultural Labor Force, and Growth in Agriculture

Dependent Variable	Time Lag	TotInvMin	LoDevel x HiConcen x TotInvMin	HiDevel x HiConcen x TotInvMin	Pop	AgLab	R²	N
	No Lag	.00			-.08		-.03	58
			.04		-.08		-.03	58
				-.12	-.11		-.01	58
AgLab	Three Year	-.03			.03		-.03	61
			.10		.04		-.02	61
				-.16	.00		.00	61
	Six Year	-.04			.03		-.03	61
			.10		.04		-.02	61
				-.16	.00		-.01	61
	Nine Year	-.20			-.20		.02	54
			.09		-.13		-.01	54
				-.23	-.18		.03	54
	No Lag	.22			.29*	.02	.04	58
			-.26		.22	.03	.06	58
				.27*	.27*	.05	.07	58
Growth in Agr.	Three Year	.10			.08	.27*	.03	61
			.21		.05	.24	.07	61
				.12	.07	.28*	.04	61
	Six Year	.03			.00	-.40**	.12	61
			-.02		.00	-.40**	.12	61
				-.17	-.04	-.43***	.14	61
	Nine Year	.14			.26	-.06	.02	54
			-.09		.22	-.08	.01	54
				.09	.24	-.07	.01	54

*p<.05
**p<.01
***p<.001

and more dependent countries, where the potential addition to local resource availability would be greatest. Such countries, however, were regarded as lacking the local support structures and the needed bargaining leverage with the multinational corporation to push for the ongoing contributions required for continuing growth. As a result, the expectation was that such growth as occurred would be ephemeral. The results conformed to these projections.

Mining investment had a similar short-lived effect on growth. Again, it was projected that the greatest impact would be on the manufacturing sector in poor and dependent states. In the case of mining investments, the inability of host governments to regulate the international marketing of the commodities mined in their countries was regarded as the key to the lack of long-term growth. The results of the analysis supported these arguments. Mining investments were associated with higher immediate growth, followed by lower growth in manu-

Table 4.24
Investments in Manufacturing and Growth in Agriculture, Controlling for Growth in Manufacturing and in Transportation and Communications

Time Lag	TotInvMan	LoDevel x HiConcen x TotInvMan	HiDevel x HiConcen x TotInvMan	Pop	Man	TC	R²	N
No	.08			.22	.07		.00	62
Lag		-.04		.19	.11		.00	62
			.12	.22	.10		.01	62
Three	.23			.12	.18		.02	68
Year		.09		.08	.13		-.02	68
			.00	.07	.10		-.03	68
Six	-.07			-.07	.22		.01	67
Year		.01		-.05	.22		.00	67
			-.14	-.07	.23		.02	67
Nine	-.36**			.12	.24*		.15	61
Year		-.44***		.16	.28*		.21	61
			.13	.24	.19		.04	61
No	-.12			.13		-.07	-.01	61
Lag		-.25		.14		-.07	.05	61
			.10	.18		-.06	-.01	61
Three	.29*			.10		.37**	.15	67
Year		.11		.04		.35**	.09	67
			.00	.03		.34**	.08	67
Six	-.20			-.06		.02	-.01	66
Year		-.11		-.01		.02	-.03	66
			-.13	-.03		.02	-.03	66
Nine	-.11			.17		.02	.00	59
Year		-.22		.18		.01	.04	59
			.12	.22		.02	.00	59

*p<.05
**p<.01
***p<.001

facturing (when the masking effects of governmental management were controlled for).

Growth in agriculture was also affected by foreign investment as much as was expected. Flows of foreign investment seem to assist higher agricultural growth indirectly by way of a contribution to growth in modern sectors, especially the transportation and communications sector. There was no association between foreign investment and changes in the agricultural labor force. Foreign investment in manufacturing was related to a higher level of governmental management, which in turn was related to lower agricultural growth; however, the results from previous chapters suggest that while foreign investments may augment governmental strength over time, they do not have any significant effect upon the priorities the government sets for using that strength. The findings from this analysis imply that the host government's preferences strongly favor using ad-

Table 4.25

Investments in Mining and Growth in Agriculture, Controlling for Growth in Manufacturing and in Transportation and Communications

Time Lag	TotInvMin	LoDevel x HiConcen x TotInvMin	HiDevel x HiConcen x TotInvMin	Pop	Man	TC	R^2	N
No	.23			.29*	.06		.05	57
Lag		-.28*		.22	.10		.07	57
			.27*	.27*	.04		.07	57
Three	.06			.03	.20		.00	61
Year		.42**		-.04	.40**		.14	61
			.06	.02	.20		.00	61
Six	-.01			-.06	.20		-.01	61
Year		-.04		-.05	.19		-.01	61
			-.11	-.07	.20		.00	61
Nine	.14			.29*	.10		.04	55
Year		-.09		.24	.12		.03	55
			.11	.27	.12		.03	55
No	.24			.30*		-.01	.04	55
Lag		-.27*		.21		-.02	.07	55
			.28*	.28*		-.02	.08	55
Three	.09			.03		.27*	.03	60
Year		.26*		.00		.29*	.09	60
			.05	.00		.27*	.03	60
Six	.06			.00		.02	-.05	60
Year		-.06		-.01		.02	-.05	60
			-.10	-.03		.02	-.04	60
Nine	.18			.30*		.04	.03	53
Year		-.10		.24		.03	.01	53
			.12	.27		.03	.01	53

*p<.05
**p<.01

ditional resource availability to promote the manufacturing sector to the detriment of agricultural output.

In conclusion, the primary effects of multinational corporations upon growth in underdeveloped societies seem to stem from the degree to which their investments add to resource availability in the host country. The potential for contributing significantly to resource availability is highest in very poor and dependent societies. These are the very countries, however, that have the least to offer foreign investors, that have the poorest support facilities, and that have little strength to use when negotiating with multinational firms to seek to compel them to make longer-term contributions to local economic growth. The result is that while initial growth does occur, it dies out after a short while. Thus, one confronts the paradox that the very countries where foreign firms are most likely to be able to aid development are those where they are least likely to have an interest in doing so and where governments are unable to force them to do so.

Given these results, one must conclude that in the absence of both improved strength leading to a better bargaining position for the host government and a greater emphasis upon creating the local conditions that will create an ongoing interest by foreigners in the host country, foreign investments have little to contribute over the long term to growth in very poor and dependent countries. In other words, as Jackman (1982:185–87) notes, wealth is the key to ongoing development and growth. Countries that are relatively well developed may expect an active interest by multinational firms. The results pertaining to the tendency of future flows of investment to be directed toward wealthier states with higher past flows support this contention. These wealthier countries, however, are precisely the ones that appear to benefit the least from the additional resources added by multinational activities. Poorer countries that could benefit the most appear to hold little interest over time for foreigners, and host government attempts to create the sorts of conditions that will interest multinational corporations must by necessity involved substantial development, which is precisely the goal the host government seeks the assistance of foreigners to meet. Moreover, once conditions are created to sufficiently interest multinational firms, the contribution of the latter to local development seems to become superfluous.

Hence, one must conclude that while multinational corporations do not seem to display many of the distasteful characteristics that alliance (both asymmetrical and symmetrical) and malevolence theorists attribute to them, neither do they make the important contributions to growth and development that liberals project. Instead, such firms appear to pursue their self-interest. On occasion, the pursuit of corporate self-interest contributes incidentally to local growth. Rarely does a multinational presence appear to harm the local economy decisively. Host governments see to that as they pursue their preferred goals. For the most part, however, foreign firms to not appear to offer the plethora of benefits that many hope for.

NOTES

1. Gobalet and Diamond (1979) do employ time-lagged analysis, but the measures used for the independent and dependent variables make a sufficient test of the effects of stocks and flows difficult. The operationalization of foreign investment used, debits on investment income, is regarded by Bornschier et al. (1978:661) as a measure of stocks. No measure of flows was included in the analysis. Moreover, the dependent variable examined was the logarithm of per capita GNP instead of some measure of real economic growth.

Rothgeb (1984a, 1984–85) does use a time-lagged design of the sort discussed in Chapter 2. However, as shall be seen, this research is plagued by the lack of careful path analysis that seeks to specify the precise causal mechanisms by which foreign investment affects host economy growth.

Interestingly, despite their severe criticism of the time periods employed in Jackman's (1982) research, Bornschier and Chase-Dunn (1985:86) fail to employ the time-lagged design needed to test properly their theoretical contentions. These authors analyze the growth occurring between 1965 and 1977, basing their measure of growth on the difference between these two years in the value of GNP per capita (see Bornschier and Chase-Dunn, 1985:63). This sort of growth measure creates two types of problems. The first is that it covers such a lengthy amount of time that specific developments that may occur during subsets of time within the overall period are obfuscated. Within any period as long as twelve years, one may expect countries to experience relatively higher and lower levels of growth. Using a twelve-year average makes it impossible to consider the relationship of foreign investment to these developments. A second is that the use of a twelve-year average makes it impossible to test for the possible short- and long-term effects of foreign investment (see Rothgeb, 1984–85:7). An effort is made to correct these difficulties in the present analysis.

2. Other methodological difficulties also plague past research. One is multicollinearity. As noted in Chapter 2, the multiple regression results that one obtains may be severely affected if two or more of the independent variables in the regression equation are related to one another. Yet, one finds on occasion no indication by researchers that this problem has been addressed. One example is the work of Bornschier and Chase-Dunn (1985:95), where the following seven independent variables are included in a single regression equation: total stock of foreign investment, total flows, the logarithm of GNP per captia, the logarithm of GNP per capita squared, domestic investment, exports, and the logarithm of energy consumption. The results found in Rothgeb's (1986a, 1986b) research imply strongly that such an equation may be seriously affected by multicollinearity, as suggested also by the preliminary findings associated with the work reported in Chapters 2 and 3 of this book.

Bornschier and Chase-Dunn (1985) also illustrate another basic problem. This pertains to missing data. These authors fail to indicate how they handled situations in which data were not available for countries that they wished to include in their study. Two commonly used techniques are to perform the analysis only upon countries for which data are complete (see Rothgeb, 1986a:132) and to substitute the mean value of the variable for all missing cases. Vincent (1980:382) discusses the first of these techniques as preferable, noting that the use of mean values may severely distort the results of the analysis. As noted in Chapter 2, the former procedure is employed in this book.

3. As has been discussed, the actual ability of an underdeveloped government to control behavior within its territory is a product of its strength and the strength of the entity it wishes to control (see Biersteker, 1980:207–21).

4. It should be noted that the measurement of flows used in this research (see Chapter 2 for a discussion of the measurement procedure) represents the degree to which corporate operations are expanded. As a result, the measure incorporates three components of corporate behavior: (1) inflows of capital from abroad, (2) the reinvestment of the profits from local operations, and (3) borrowing on local credit markets. Consequently, tests of hypotheses regarding flows of investments actually examine the overall expansion of corporate operations. Limitations pertaining to data availability force the use of this sort of measure upon the researcher (see Rothgeb, 1986a:133; 1986b:147). Indeed, Bornschier et al. (1978), Bornschier (1981), and Bornschier and Chase-Dunn (1985) employ the same types of measures for flows. Fortunately, the theoretical structure of the argument regarding change in flows presented both by Bornschier and Chase-Dunn and in the present research pertain quite nicely whether one narrowly considers change in flows or more broadly concerns oneself with the general expansion of corporate operations (by whatever method).

5. One may recall the discussion in Chapter 3 that posited a positive association

between flows and resource availability in the host state (particularly in very poor and dependent countries). The current expectation that there will be no relationship between flows (as measured with currently available procedures) and growth in domestic investment does not contradict this earlier argument for precisely the same reason that the positive relationship between growth and flows is not ruled out by the lack of an expected association between flows and growth in domestic investment. A high level of flows represents an expansion of the foreign presence in the host society and increased economic activity. This produces more resources and should be associated with greater growth. Much (but not all) of this economic activity is a product of the employment of local capital. Thus, one has greater resource availability and economic growth without any clear effect on growth in domestic investment.

6. Manufacturing firms that produce goods for export are an exception. As Reuber (1973) and Frank (1980) discuss, however, manufacturing subsidiaries of this sort are a minority of the total foreign manufacturing firms found in developing states. The analysis of the differing roles played by market penetration and export-oriented manufacturing firms, although an important subject of concern, is hindered by the lack of a data base that allows one to distinguish between these two types of investments.

7. This is not meant to suggest that profits are unavailable. Instead, the argument is based on the premise that the key to *growth* is an *ever-expanding* investment pool. An ever-expanding investment pool requires a constant *increase* in profits that are then plowed back as reinvestments. It is doubtful that the expansion in profits occurring in very poor and dependent societies is sufficient to promote the increase in reinvestments that would be needed to promote continually higher rates of growth. Instead, it is expected that manufacturing investments will lead to an *absolute* increase in local resource availability of the sort required to promote short-term growth and more local social reform (see Chapter 3) but that a constant expansion in resources of the sort needed to have consistent increases in resources (and growth) will not be possible.

8. It should be recalled once again that these arguments do *not* mean that an *absolute* increase in the availability of foreign exchange does not occur. It does, and is used, as was found in Chapter 3, to promote domestic reform. The key argument here is the same as in note 6 above: the promotion of ongoing *growth* requires a constantly expanding foreign exchange pool. While such an expansion may occur early on, it is doubtful that it is continual.

9. Figures for gross domestic product were used in preference to figures for gross national product because GNP includes "net factor income received from abroad" (World Bank, 1976:6), which includes the income of a state's citizens derived from their activities in other countries and excludes noncitizens' income that is remitted abroad. Hence, GNP figures partially represent productive efforts found in *other* economies and exclude a portion of the productive effort found in the economy in question. However, GDP represents the total value of "all goods produced and services rendered within (a state's) territory by residents and non-residents" (World Bank, 1976:5) and therefore may be conceptualized as a better representation of the effects of foreign investment upon the economic performance of the territory found within the host state's sovereign jurisdiction. Growth rates for total GDP were used instead of figures for growth in GDP per capital because, as Mahler (1980:74) points out, growth in GDP per capital is based both upon the increase (or decrease) in the production of goods and services and upon the growth in a state's population. For the most part, the theoretical arguments found in the literature focus only upon the former and rarely attribute (either implicitly or explicitly) the host

state's population growth rate to multinational corporate activities. Thus, the use of growth in total GDP appears most reasonable.

10. In order to determine whether the use of a combined total stock figure affected the results, the analysis was replicated using the measures employed in Chapters 2 and 3 for stocks of foreign investment. In each case, the results were the same as those that are reported.

11. Gross domestic fixed capital formation was used in preference to gross domestic investment or gross domestic capital formation because the latter two figures include the increase in stock of inventory produced by domestic industries (World Bank, 1976:7). Increase in stock of inventory does not have the same impact on future growth as does fixed capital formation (Spencer, 1974:131–32). Of course, data that compensated for depreciation would have been better, but such data are available for very few countries. In addition, figures for domestic investment according to sector, although preferable for the present analysis, generally are not available. Therefore, gross domestic fixed capital formation was used as substitute.

12. Once again, the reader is reminded that this comment is not intended to mean that all of the relationships were linear.

13. The reader should recall that this analysis deals with growth *rates* and not with *absolute* growth. These results suggest that foreign manufacturing investment produces a higher initial rate of growth. This higher growth results in a larger *absolute* amount of production that is the base for computing all future *rates* of growth. Thus, the greater initial growth creates a new absolute standard against which future growth is compared. Merely producing at a rate equal to that standard would result in a growth rate of zero. One must substantially exceed that standard in order to maintain the initial rate of growth occurring due to the introduction of foreign investment. The findings suggest that very poor and dependent societies lack the proper support structures to do this.

14. A note of caution is called for when interpreting the results for profits: one must reverse the signs of the beta coefficients. This is necessary because the profit figures represent the amount of total profits earned by host state–based firms abroad net the amount earned by foreign firms operating in the host state. The profit values for each country in the sample are negative numbers, and the beta signs must be reversed.

15. The reader should recall that the results reported here are for total stock of foreign investment from all sources, while the results reported in Chapter 3 were for stock of foreign investment from the single largest foreign national source.

5

Conclusions and Observations

This book has been about the role played by one of the newest international actors, the multinational corporation, in the development process in underdeveloped societies. The fundamental goal was to develop a theoretical framework for understanding how multinational corporations affect the political, social, and economic conditions found in poorer countries. Beyond this, the objective of the analysis was to assess the accuracy of claims and counterclaims found in the literature on multinational corporations to determine whether these firms do indeed have sufficient capabilities to serve as modern transnational leviathans that seriously challenge the state's position as the dominant actor in the Third World. In addition, pursuing these goals provided the opportunity to examine the impact of external forces upon underdeveloped societies and to investigate questions pertaining to the operation of one aspect of the structure of the international system, the economic linkages between rich and poor societies.

It was projected that conceptualizing the relations between multinational corporations and host states as a political contest involving asymmetrically interdependent actors would allow one to sort through some of the myths and realities regarding the impacts of foreign investment on underdeveloped countries. This approach was used to examine the effects of multinational corporations on foreign policy, domestic political and social behavior, and economic growth.

The evidence from this analysis implies very strongly that one myth regarding multinational corporations relates to the Trojan Horse–asymmetrical alliance notions that foreign firms are used to control foreign policy, to regulate domestic political and social conditions, and to stunt the growth of the economies of underdeveloped societies. Several qualifications must be attached to this statement. For one, this does not mean that the international system does not have a structure that is somewhat feudal, with a fairly clearly defined class structure of wealthier and poorer countries. Previous research by Galtung (1971), Addo (1974), and Gidengil (1978) indicate that the international arena has these characteristics. There also is little doubt that an international division of labor exists to some extent, with some countries producing for the most part primary products, while others are preponderant in the more technologically sophisticated and capital-intensive industrial area. Moreover, this research has not attempted to assess the degree to which stronger and wealthier countries use their power to dominate weaker and poorer countries. Clearly, the strong often do seek to suit their own best interests through control of the weak.

The problem addressed herein related to whether multinational corporations are a basic instrument operating systematically to perpetuate an international system of control. Expectations based upon viewing multinational corporation–host country relations as involving a series of political conflicts occurring within a framework of asymmetrical interdependence cast doubt both upon the idea that multinational firms would pursue such a course and upon the belief that host states would play the sorts of supporting roles envisioned for them. The findings indicate that conceptions based upon the Trojan Horse–asymmetrical alliance approach are inaccurate. As was discussed in earlier chapters, the sorts of behavior discussed by theorists from this school of thought should have been manifested most clearly among the poorest and most dominated members of the Third World. The expected patterns of relationships were that higher levels of foreign investment would be associated with more foreign policy cooperation and less conflict, a weaker central government, less social reform, more repression by the government, a higher repatriation of profits leading to less domestic investment, and a lower level of growth in the manufacturing sector. In no case was the expected pattern found, providing evidence based upon the analysis of several different types of behavior that multinational corporations and host governments do not act in conformity with the expectations derived from this model.

As noted in the concluding section to Chapter 2, the specific conditions found internationally and the identity of the home country from which foreign investments emanate may play a key role in determining the degree to which a Trojan Horse–asymmetrical pattern of mastery exists. Future research should address this. For now, the conclusion is that the multinational corporation is not a central actor in any international structure of control.

Another myth pertains to the liberal view that the multinational corporation is an "engine of development," constituting a force for progress that creates interdependence leading to increasing international cooperation and greater domestic tranquility. According to this conception, foreign firms introduce new values that temper the rough edges of underdeveloped host governments, encouraging them to extend social reforms to the people and to ease up on repressive rule. At the same time, such corporations spur local economic growth and development by bringing with them important factors of production that are missing in poor societies, resulting in the stimulation of domestic investment, a greater and more effective role for the government in promoting the expansion of the economy, and a vigorous and ongoing pattern of growth in all sectors, both traditional and modern, of the host economy.

Again, projections based upon competitive asymmetrical interdependence cast doubt upon these views. To a large extent, it would appear that the liberal conception gives the multinational corporation false credit for many of the benefits that are associated with the modernization process in general, instead of with the foreign corporate activities in particular. In other words, the relationships are spurious. The findings in this book imply that foreign firms do not affect the policy preferences of host governments and that they have little desire to attempt to exert such effects, except under the most limited circumstances. In addition, host governments are loath to do anything to contribute to the impression that they are susceptible for foreign influences. As far as growth is concerned, foreign corporate contributions are limited and are tied closely to the corporate ability to make profits. This means that corporate activities may provide some initial benefits, especially in the manufacturing sector, but that it is the ability of the host society to magnify those inputs that creates the basis for longer-term growth and for spillover effects upon growth in other sectors of the host economy.

While liberal thinkers tend to credit foreign investments incorrectly for many of the benefits of the modernization process, malevolence theorists wrongly blame multinational corporations for many of the unpleasant aspects of the process and for much of the unfortunate behavior found in poor countries. For example, foreign investors are treated as responsible, either directly or indirectly, for such things as closed political systems, governmental repression, the absence of social reform, the migration of rural workers to urban areas where they become unemployed beggars, decaptialization through the excessive repatriation of profits, encouraging an excessive consumption of foreign-made luxury goods that results in lower domestic investment, and the absence of a long-term pattern of continuing economic growth and development. The foregoing analysis indicates that while many of these problems do plague underdeveloped countries, for the most part multinational corporations play little role in their creation. Once again, the suspected relationship between foreign investments and these sorts of problems is spurious. Juxtaposing the general absence of many of the expected malevolent effects with the lack of a systematic liberalizing impact suggests that while foreign investments cannot be held responsible for many of the difficulties found in underdeveloped countries, neither do they provide much assistance in solving these problems.

The symmetrical alliance between foreign investors and the host government in wealthier underdeveloped host countries is somewhat more difficult to judge. On the one hand, the notion that the multinational corporation and the host government enjoy close relations and try to use one another in a symbiotic association designed to further the ability of each to meet its preferred goals is consistent with the arguments and findings herein. On the other hand, the projection that this relationship leads to an overbearing role for the government resulting in less social reform, more repression, and an emphasis on growth in manufacturing seems somewhat wide of the mark. Foreign investment appears to have few of these effects in wealthier Third World states. Governments do appear to stress the manufacturing sector and may be overbearing, but there is good reason to believe that this is done without any reference to the desires of foreign investors. In addition, stock of foreign investment has no effect on growth in manufacturing in such countries. Of course, it is possible that foreign investment only affects the part of the local industrial establishment that engages in technologically sophisticated production and that a measure for overall growth in manufacturing, such as was used in this study, is too inexact to capture such an impact. Future research should address this possibility. For the present, however, the conclusion is that a symmetrical alliance of the sort discussed in the literature does not seem to exist.

In place of the above conceptions, one might present a different picture. As far as the role of the multinational corporation is concerned, the results imply that such firms are not the sort of leviathans described in much of the literature. The multinational corporation is just one important actor among several in the context found in underdeveloped countries. While the corporation is stronger than some actors, it is not omnipotent. It operates within the specific constraints imposed by the state, even when that state is weak. That is, the multinational corporation seems to play the role of a powerful interest group, acting to protect its interests, which center on making profits, and having little concern in general for the interests of others, whether it is the home government, the host government, domestic interest groups, or other multinational firms. Foreign investors appear to try to avoid involvement in local foreign or domestic policy and politics, except when their own interests are involved directly. The multinational corporation as an institution appears to have no systematic interest either in helping or in hurting the host economy.

As a result of these attitudes, the multinational corporation does not interest itself in the development of a close alliance with the local elite. Such firms simply are uninterested in paying the upkeep on such arrangements, are loath to accept the risks associated with the participation in the local political scene that an alliance would involve, and are uninterested in taking part in assisting others in the pursuit of goals that often are only of tangential importance to the firm.

The greatest source of strength for the foreign firm in underdeveloped countries may result from the perceptions that host government officials have as to the potential benefits that may result from foreign investments. Such perceptions also serve as the source of some of the firm's greatest problems. The firm frequently is regarded as an important international source of capital, technology, and entrepreneurial ability, and therefore is believed to be a key to rapid growth and development. These beliefs are most pronounced when the host state is very poor and dependent and when the corporation's operations are in manufacturing. The result is a pattern of asymmetrical interdependence that might appear on the surface to give the corporation substantial advantages over the host country.

Limits exist, however, to restrain the firm. The most important of these is the suspicion with which foreigners are viewed. Suspicion results from the local fear of foreign exploitation and domination and the resultant loss of autonomy that is associated with a large foreign presence. These emotions appear to be keenly felt and are ubiquitous, found even in the wealthiest Third World states, which apparently have the least to fear from multinational corporations. Thus, foreign investments both may be heralded as a possible champion of development and at the same time may be the subject of veiled hostility.

One outgrowth of these impulses is increased political conflict, particularly in wealthier countries where mining investments are regarded as akin to the basest exploitation and where manufacturing investments seem to lead to the fear of foreign control over the most vital and progressive segment of the host economy. A second outgrowth is the lack of any extensive foreign policy co-operation that would serve to create greater ties of interdependence with the foreign investor's home state. Increased ties of this sort appear to be associated with the loss of autonomy and independence of action in the international arena and with too great a domestic role for foreigners in the host country.

Another effect of the attitude of suspicion toward foreign investors is scape-goating. Scapegoating occurs when a feeling of exploitation is coupled with disillusionment at the lack of local progress in development and with the per-ception that such behavior involves no cost because of a lack of vulnerability to foreign investors. As the findings in Chapter 2 show, scapegoating centers on foreign investments in mining, which are regarded as exploitative. While these investments produce growth in manufacturing, as Chapter 4 shows, these benefits are ephemeral, contributing both to disillusionment and frustration and to the feeling that one has little to lose in attacking the foreigners. Thus, the latent suspicion and hostility felt toward the multinational corporation comes to the forefront and conflict occurs.

The inherent suspicion of host government officials toward foreign corpora-tions inclines the host government to use the firm to meet its goals whenever possible. As mentioned elsewhere, the basic objective for the government is to strengthen its position in society to ensure its grasp on power. This may be accomplished by increasing the economic well-being of the people and providing them with services that will enhance the government's image as legitimate. Foreign investments apparently are perceived as having the potential for aiding the government in these endeavors, especially in very poor and dependent coun-tries.

In such societies, the evidence from this research indicates that investments both in manufacturing and in mining are associated early on with higher levels of growth in manufacturing. With mining investments, the results from Chapters 3 and 4 suggest that from the beginning the government uses the revenues from commodity sales abroad both to promote growth in the highly valued manufac-turing sector and to finance social reform.

The relationships for investments in manufacturing are somewhat different.

Here the government appears more hesitant to try to force foreigners to contribute to its goals than it does when dealing with mining investors. The varying effects of asymmetrical interdependence and the differing degrees to which investments in mining and in manufacturing are regarded by the host government as exploitative appear to account for this hesitation toward manufacturing investors. The pattern for manufacturing investments is for the greater growth found early on in the manufacturing sector to increase the absolute availability of resources. Over time, these resources are then appropriated by the state to strengthen the government's position in society and to create social reforms.

The absence of a continuing longer-term association between foreign investment and growth in manufacturing in very poor and dependent societies was explained above as being in part a result of the lack of sufficient local support facilities that are capable of magnifying the initial foreign contribution. Juxtaposing the results from Chapters 3 and 4 points to another possible reason. This is the tendency for governments in very poor and dependent societies to channel resources toward their most pressing needs, which include strengthening the government and building support among the people. In this context, appropriating resources to use in promoting reforms promises a potential immediate payoff. Using resources to encourage further growth, even in the cherished manufacturing sector, is a longer-term strategy with payoffs that only occur in the distant future if and when an expanding economy leads to more jobs and other benefits. Given the pressing nature of the problems confronting the government, one might expect that officials are unwilling to accept the risks associated with waiting and that they point resources as they become available toward the implementation of a strategy that promises more immediate returns.

In other words, the introduction of reform and the promotion of growth are means to an end. They are alternative strategies that the government in a very poor and dependent society may use for cementing its grasp on power. Given a paucity of resources, they are competing strategies; pursuing one tends to eliminate the possibility of implementing the other. In particular, the pursuit of growth in the context of poverty found in very poor Third World states requires a single-minded plowing of resources into the chosen task. Diverting resources to finance reforms may undermine decisively the ability to create continuing growth. Hence, the government's attempt to obtain a more immediate payoff in terms of support from the people may be a key element that tends to foreclose the possibility of any longer-term relationship between foreign investment and growth. Future research should focus carefully upon this possibility.

This picture is both encouraging and discouraging to those interested in helping underdeveloped countries. It is encouraging because multinational corporations appear to stimulate greater growth and provide resources for more social reform, with these impacts being greatest where they are most needed—among the least developed members of the Third World. Aside from the effect upon political conflict, the presence or absence of foreign investment seems to affect wealthier Third World states very little. The discouraging aspect of the above portrait is that multinational corporations appear very much tied to profit making and apparently are not at all inclined toward acting as any sort of international welfare or relief agency. Hence, while multinational corporations may have the ability to help very poor countries, the evidence suggests that they do not seek to do so in any systematic manner.

The basic conundrum revolves around the magnification and reinforcement of such positive effects as the multinational corporation has. At the same time, as was noted in the concluding section of Chapter 4, it must be realized that the reliance upon inputs from foreign investments for the promotion of development basically may be the equivalent of pursuing a chimera. The key to the prospects of poorer underdeveloped countries most probably centers on the policy selections of the host government. It is the government that must shoulder the extremely difficult task of foregoing the reliance upon popular shorter-term measures in favor of possibly more painful longer-term policies. What makes this so untoward for the governments of poor societies are the twin problems associated with the lack of certainty regarding longer-term payoffs and the often-found absence of a climate of sufficient toleration of political failure to permit the survival of governments that pursue long-range strategies.

Under these circumstances, it is not surprising that leaders in underdeveloped countries focus so much attention on multinational corporations. The analysis from this book suggests strongly that depending upon the multinational corporation for growth and development is misguided. Given this, and considering the pressures confronting governments in Third World societies, it should be no surprise that foreign investments are the targets of such frustration and controversy.

Appendixes

Appendix 1
States in the Data Set

Afghanistan	El Salvador	Madagascar	Singapore
Algeria	Ethiopia	Malawi	Somalia
Angola	Ghana	Malaysia	Spain
Argentina	Greece	Mali	Sri Lanka
Bangladesh	Guatemala	Mauritania	Sudan
Benin	Guinea	Mexico	Syria
Bolivia	Haiti	Mongolia	Tanzania
Burkina Faso	Honduras	Morocco	Thailand
Burma	Hong Kong	Mozambique	Togo
Burundi	India	Nicaragua	Trinidad
Cambodia	Indonesia	Niger	Tunisia
Cameroon	Iran	Nigeria	Turkey
Central African Republic	Iraq	Pakistan	Uganda
Chad	Ireland	Papua New Guinea	Uruguay
Chile	Ivory Coast	Paraguay	Venezuela
Colombia	Jamaica	Peru	Yemen North
Costa Rica	Jordan	Philippines	Yemen (South)
Dominican Republic	Kenya	Portugal	Yugoslavia
Ecuador	Korea (South)	Rwanda	Zaire
Egypt	Laos	Senegal	Zambia
	Lebanon	Sierra Leone	Zimbabwe

Appendix 2
Data Sources

Variable	Indicator	Source
Stock of foreign investment	Measured in U.S. $ for 1967, 1973, 1975, and 1978	1, 2, 3
Total stock of foreign investment from the largest foreign national source	Measured in U.S. $ for 1967	1
Total stock of foreign investment in manufacturing and in mining	Measured in U.S. $ for 1967	1
Stock of foreign investment in manufacturing and in mining from the largest foreign national source	Measured in U.S. $ for 1967	1
Proportion of total stock of foreign investment from the largest foreign national source	Measured for 1967	1
Proportion of stock of foreign investment in manufacturing and in mining from the largest foreign national source	Measured for 1967	1
Flow of foreign investment	Average annual real percentage change in total stock of foreign investment for 1967–71, 1971–73, 1973–75, and 1975–78.	1, 2, 3
Net direct investment income	Measured in U.S. $ for 1967–69	4
Foreign policy cooperation and conflict	Measured for 1967–69, 1970–72, 1973–75, and 1976–78	5
Domestic political conflict, reform and repression	Measured for 1967–69, 1970–72, 1973–75, and 1976–78	6
Total government expenditures	Measured in U.S. $ for 1967, 1970, 1973, and 1976	7

Variable	Indicator	Source
Growth in manufacturing, transportation and communications, and agriculture	Average annual real percentage change for 1967–69, 1970–72, 1973–75, and 1976–78	8
Total GDP	Measured in U.S. $ for 1967, 1970, 1973, and 1976	8
Total GDP in manufacturing and in mining	Measured in U.S. $ for 1967	8
GDP per capita	Measured in U.S. $ for 1967	8
Growth in gross domestic fixed capital formation	Average annual real percentage change for 1967–69, 1970–72, 1973–75, and 1976–78	8
Total external public debt	Measured in U.S. $ for 1967–69, 1970–72, 1973–75, and 1976–78	4
Percentage of the total labor force employed in agriculture	Measured for 1965, 1970, 1975, and 1980	4
Total population	Measured at midyear for 1967, 1970, 1973, and 1976	9

1 = OECD, "Stock of Private Direct Investment by DAC Countries in Developing Countries, Update." Paris: OECD, microfiche, no date.

2 = OECD, "Estimate of the Stock of Direct Private Investment of DAC Members in Developing Countries, End 1975." Paris: OECD, mimeo, no date.

3 = OECD, International Investment and Multinational Enterprises. *Recent International Direct Investment Trends*. Paris: OECD, 1981.

4 = World Bank, *World Tables*, 1976, 1980, 1983 editions.

5 = *Conflict and Peace Data Bank International Scale*.

6 = *Conflict and Peace Data Bank Domestic Scale*.

7 = U.S. Arms Control and Disarmament Agency, *World Military Expenditures and Arms Transfers*, various years.

8 = UN, *Yearbook of National Accounts Statistics*, vol. 2, various years.

9 = UN, *Demographic Yearbook*, various years.

References

Addo, H. 1974. "Structural Basis of International Communication." *Papers of the Peace Science Society* 23:81–100.

Adorno, T. W., E. Frenkel-Brunswik, D. J. Levinson, and R. W. Sanford. 1969. *The Authoritarian Personality*. New York: W. W. Norton.

Apter, D. E. 1976. "Charters, Cartels, and Multinationals: Some Colonial and Imperial Questions." In *The Multinational Corporation and Social Change*, edited by D. E. Apter and L. W. Goodman, 1–39. New York: Praeger.

Armstrong, A. 1981. "Political Consequences of Economic Dependence." *Journal of Conflict Resolution* 25 (September): 401–28.

Asher, H. B. 1976. *Causal Modeling*. Beverly Hills, Calif.: Sage.

Azar, E. 1980. "The Conflict and Peace Data Bank (COPDAB), Project." *Journal of Conflict Resolution* 24 (March): 143–52.

———. 1982. *The Codebook of the Conflict and Peace Data Bank*. College Park, Md.: Center for International Development. Mimeo.

Baran, P. A. 1957. *The Political Economy of Growth*. New York: Monthly Review Press.

Barnet, R. J., and R. E. Muller. 1974. *Global Reach*. New York: Simon and Schuster.

Bergeson, A. 1977. "Political Witch Hunts: The Sacred and the Subversive in Cross-National Perspective." *American Sociological Review* 42: 220–33.

Biersteker, T. J. 1980. "The Illusion of State Power: Transnational Corporations and the Neutralization of Host-Country Legislation." *Journal of Peace Research* 17: 207–221.

Bodenheimer, S. 1971. "Dependency and Imperialism: The Roots of Latin American Underdevelopment." In *Readings in U.S. Imperialism*, edited by K. T. Fann and D. C. Hodges. Boston: Porter Sargent.

Bonazzi, G. 1983. "Scapegoating in Complex Organizations: The Results of a Comparative Study of Symbolic Blame-Giving in Italian and French Public Administration." *Organization Studies* 4: 1–18.

Bornschier, V. 1981. "Dependent Industrialization in the Economy." *Journal of Conflict Resolution* 25 (September): 371–400.

Bornschier, V., and T. Ballmer-Cao. 1979. "Income Inequality: A Cross-National Study of the Relationship Betwen MNC Penetration, Dimensions of the Power Structure, and Income Distribution." *American Sociological Review* 44 (June): 487–506.

Bornschier, V., and C. Chase-Dunn. 1985. *Transnational Corporations and Underdevelopment*. New York: Praeger.

Bornschier, V., C. Chase-Dunn, and R. Rubinson. 1978. "Cross-National Evidence of the Effects of Foreign Investment and Aid on Economic Growth and Inequality: A Survey of Findings and a Reanalysis." *American Journal of Sociology* 84 (November): 651–83.

Brundenius, C. 1972. "The Anatomy of Imperialism: The Case of Multinational Mining Corporations in Peru." *Journal of Peace Research* 9: 189–207.

Bueno de Mesquita, B. 1985. "Toward a Scientific Understanding of International Conflict: A Personal View." *International Studies Quarterly* 29 (June): 121–36.

Burgess, M., and R. W. Lawton. 1975. "Evaluating Events Data: Problems of Conception, Reliability, and Validity." In *International Events and the Comparative Analysis of Foreign Policy*, edited by C. W. Kegley, Jr., G. A. Raymond, R. M. Rood, and R. A. Skinner, 106–119. University of South Carolina Press.

Caporaso, J. A. 1978a. "Dependence, Dependency, and Power in the Global System: A Structural and Behavioral Analysis." *International Organization* 32 (Winter): 13–43.

———. 1978b. "Introduction." *International Organization* 32 (Winter): 1–12.

———. 1980. "Dependency Theory: Continuities and Discontinuities in Development Studies." *International Organization* 34 (Autumn): 605–28.

Cardoso, F. H., and E. Faletto. 1979. *Dependency and Development in Latin America*. Berkeley, Calif.: University of California Press.

Chase-Dunn, C. 1975. "The Effects of International Economic Dependence on Development and Inequality: A Cross-National Study." *American Sociological Review* 40: 720–38.

———. 1978. "Core-Periphery Relations: The Effects of Core Competition." In *Social Change in the Capitalist World Economy*, edited by B. H. Kaplan, 159–76. Beverly Hills, Ca.: Sage.

Chase-Dunn, C. and R. Rubinson. 1977. "Toward a Structural Perspective on the World System." *Politics and Society* 7: 453–76.

———. 1979. "Cycles, Trends, and New Departures in World System Development." In *National Development and the World System*, edited by J. W. Meyer and M. T. Hannan, 276–96. Chicago: University of Chicago Press.

Chenery, H., and M. Syrquin. 1975. *Patterns of Development*. New York: Oxford University Press.

Claude, I. L., Jr. 1971. *Swords into Plowshares*. New York: Random House.

Cohen, B. J. 1973. *The Question of Imperialism*. New York: Basic Books.

Diaz-Alejandro, C. F. 1970. "Direct Foreign Investment in Latin America." In *The International Corporation*, edited by C. P. Kindleberger, 319–44. Cambridge, Mass.: MIT Press.

Dolan, M., and B. W. Tomlin. 1980. "First World–Third World Linkages: External Relations and Economic Development." *International Organization* 34 (Winter): 41–64.

Dolan, M., B. W. Tomlin, H. Von Riekhoff, and M. A. Molot. 1982. "Asymmetrical Dyads and Foreign Policy: Canada-U.S. Relations, 1963–72." *Journal of Conflict Resolution* 26 (September): 387–422.

Dos Santos, T. 1971. "The Strucutre of Dependence." In *Readings in U.S. Imperialism*, edited by K. T. Fann and D. C. Hodges, 225–36. Boston: Porter Sargent.

Duvall, R. D., and J. R. Freeman. 1981. "The State and Dependent Capitalism." *International Studies Quarterly* 25 (March): 99–118.

———. 1983. "The Techno-Bureaucratic Elite and the Entrepreneurial State in Dependent Industrialization." *American Political Science Review* 77 (September): 569–87.

Eagle, J., and P. M. Newton. 1981. "Scapegoating in Small Groups: An Organizational Approach." *Human Relations* 34: 283–301.

East, M. A. 1973. "Size and Foreign Policy Behavior: A Test of Two Models." *World Politics* 25: 556–76.

Evans, P. 1971. "National Autonomy and Economic Development: Critical Perspectives on Multinational Corporations in Poor Countries." In *Transnational Relations and World Politics*, edited by R. O. Keohane and J.S. Nye, Jr., 325–42. Cambridge, Mass.: Harvard University Press.

———. 1979. *Dependent Development*. Princeton, N.J.: Princeton University Press.

Evans, P., and M. Timberlake. 1980. "Dependence, Inequality, and Growth in the Tertiary: A Comparative Analysis of Less Developed Countries." *American Sociological Review* 45: 531–52.

Fagen, R. R. 1978. "A Funny Thing Happened on the Way to the Market: Thoughts on Extending Dependency Ideas." *International Organization* 32 (Winter): 287–300.

Fieldhouse, D. K. 1978. *Unilever Overseas: The Anatomy of a Multinational, 1895–1965*. London: Croom Helm.

Fleet, M. H. 1982. "The Politics of Auto Industry Development in Colombia." *Journal of InterAmerican Studies and World Affairs* 24 (May): 211–39.

Frank, A. G. 1969. *Latin America: Underdevelopment or Revolution*. New York: Monthly Review Press.

Frank, I. 1980. *Foreign Enterprise in Developing Countries*. Baltimore: Johns Hopkins University Press.

Frieden, J. 1981. "Third World Indebted Industrialization: International Finance and State Capitalism in Mexico, Brazil, Algeria, and South Korea." *International Organization* 35 (Summer): 407–32.

Galeano, E. 1971. "Latin America and the Theory of Imperialism." In *Readings in U.S. Imperialism*, edited by K. T. Fann and D. C. Hodges, 205–24. Boston: Porter Sargent.

Galtung, J. 1971. "A Structural Theory of Imperialism." *Journal of Peace Research* 8 (no. 2): 81–117.

Gereffi, G. 1978. "Drugs Firms and Dependency in Mexico: The Case of the Steroid Hormone Industry." *International Organization* 32 (Winter): 237–86.

Gidengil, E. L. 1978. "Centers and Peripheries: An Empirical Test of Galtung's Theory of Imperialism." *Journal of Peace Research* 15: 51–66.

Gilpin, R. 1975. *U.S. Power and the Multinational Corporation*. New York: Basic Books.

Gobalet, J. G., and L. J. Diamond. 1979. "Effects of Investment Dependence on Economic Growth." *International Studies Quarterly* 23 (September): 412–44.

Heilbroner, R. L. 1963. *The Great Ascent*. New York: Harper Torchbooks.

Heise, D. R. 1975. *Causal Analysis*. New York: Wiley-Interscience.

Hermann, C. F. 1978. "Foreign Policy Behavior: That Which Is to Be Explained." In *Why Nations Act*, edited by M. A. East, S. A. Salmore, and C. F. Hermann, 25–48. Beverly Hills, Ca.: Sage.

Hoggard, D. D. 1974. "Differential Source Coverage in Foreign Policy Analysis." In *Comparing Foreign Policies: Theories, Findings, and Methods*, edited by J. N. Rosenau, 353–82. New York: Halsted Press.

Holsti, K. J. 1975. "Underdevelopment and the 'Gap' Theory of International Conflict." *American Political Science Review* 69: 827–39.

Hveem, H. 1973. "The Global Dominance System: Notes on a Theory of Global Political Economy." *Journal of Peace Research* 10 (no. 4): 319–40.

Jackman, R. W. 1980. "A Note on the Measurement of Growth Rates in Cross-National Research." *American Journal of Sociology* 86 (November): 604–17.

———. 1982. "Dependence on Foreign Investment and Economic Growth in the Third World." *World Politics* 34 (January): 175–96.

Jackson, S., B. Russett, D. Snidal, and D. Sylvan. 1978. "Conflict and Coercion in Dependent States." *Journal of Conflict Resolution* 22 (December): 627–58.

Jones, W. S. 1985. *The Logic of International Relations*. Boston: Little, Brown.

Kegley, C. W., Jr. 1975. "Introduction: The Generation and Use of Events Data." In *International Events and the Comparative Analysis of Foreign Policy*, edited by C. W. Kegley, Jr., et al., 91–105. Columbia: University of South Carolina Press.

Keohane, R. O., and J. S. Nye. 1977. *Power and Interdependence*. Boston: Little, Brown.

Keohane, R. O., and V. D. Ooms. 1972. "The Multinational Enterprise and World Political Economy." *International Organization* 26 (Winter): 84–120.

Kindleberger, C. 1979. "The Monopolistic Theory of Direct Foreign Investment." In *Transnational Corporations and World Order*, edited by G. Modelski, 91–107. San Francisco: W.H. Freeman.

Krasner, S. D. 1976. "State Power and the Structure of International Trade." *World Politics* 28: 317–47.

———. 1981. "Transforming International Regimes: What the Third World Wants and Why." In *World System Structure: Continuity and Change*, edited by W.L. Hollist and J.N. Rosenau, 171–210. Beverly Hills, Calif.: Sage.

Leonard, H. J. 1980. "Multinational Corporations and Politics in Developing Countries." *World Politics* 32 (April): 454–483.

Lewis-Beck, M. S. 1980. *Applied Regression: An Introduction*. Beverly Hills, Calif.: Sage Publications.

Lim, D. 1983. "Fiscal Incentives and Direct Foreign Investment in Less Developed Countries." *Journal of Development Studies* 19: 207–12.

Lipson, C. 1981. "The International Organization of Third World Debt." *International Organization* 35 (Autumn): 603–32.

Lowe, A. 1981. "Responses of a Multinational Corporation to the Problem of Surplus Capacity." In *The International Politics of Surplus Capacity*, edited by S. Strange and R. Tooze, 150–56. London: Allen and Unwin.

McGowan, P. J. 1975. "Meaningful Comparisons in the Study of Foreign Policy: A Methodological Discussion of Objectives, Techniques, and Research Designs." In *International Events and the Comparative Analysis of Foreign Policy*, edited by, C. W. Kegley, Jr., G. A. Raymond, R. M. Rood, and R. A. Skinner, 52–87. Columbia: University of South Carolina Press.

McGowan, P. J., and D. L. Smith. 1978. "Economic Dependency in Black Africa: An Analysis of Competing Theories." *International Organization* 32 (Winter): 179–236.

Magdoff, H. 1969. *The Age of Imperialism: The Economics of U.S. Foreign Policy.* New York: Monthly Review Press.

———. 1976. "The Multinational Corporation and Development: A Contradiction?" In *The Multinational Corporation and Social Change*, edited by D. E. Apter and L. W. Goodman, 200–222. New York: Praeger.

Magdoff, H., and P. M. Sweezy. 1971. "Notes on the Multinational Corporation." In *Readings in U.S. Imperialism*, edited by K. T. Fann and D. C. Hodges, 93–116. Boston: Porter Sargent.

Mahler, V. 1980. *Dependency Approaches to International Political Economy.* New York: Columbia University Press.

———. 1981. "Mining, Agriculture, and Manufacturing: The Impact of Foreign Investment on Social Distribution in Third World Countries." *Comparative Political Studies* 14 (October): 267–97.

Markus, G. B. 1979. *Analyzing Panel Data.* Beverly Hills, Calif.: Sage.

Moon, B. E. 1983. "The Foreign Policy of the Dependent State." *International Studies Quarterly* 27 (September): 315–40.

———. 1985. "Consensus or Compliance? Foreign Policy Change and External Dependence." *International Organization* 39 (Spring): 297–330.

Moore, R. M. 1973. "Imperialism and Dependency in Latin America: A View of the New Reality of Multinational Investment." *Journal of Inter-American Studies and World Affairs* 15: 21–35.

Moran, T. H. 1974. *Multinational Corporations and the Politics of Dependence.* Princeton, N.J.: Princeton University Press.

———. 1978. "Multinational Corporations and Dependency: A Dialogue for Dependentistas and non-Dependentistas." *International Organization* 32 (Winter): 79–100.

Morgenthau, H. 1973. *Politics Among Nations.* New York: Knopf.

Morse, E. L. 1976. *Modernization and the Transformation of International Relations.* New York: Free Press.

Muller, R. 1976. "The Political Economy of Global Corporations and National Stabilization Policy: A Diagnostic on the Need for Social Planning." In *The Multinational Corporation and Social Change*, edited by D. E. Apter and L. W. Goodman, 197–99. New York: Praeger.

Nie, N.H., C.H. Hull, J. G. Jenkins, K. Steinbrenner, and D. H. Bent. 1975. *Statistical Package for the Social Sciences.* New York: McGraw-Hill.

Nye, J.S., Jr., and R. O. Keohane. 1971. "Transnational Relations and World Politics: A Conclusion." In *Transnational Relations and World Politics*, edited by R. O. Keohane and J. S. Nye, Jr., 371–98. Cambridge: Harvard University Press.

———. 1971a. "Transnational Relations and World Politics: An Introduction." In *Transnational Relations and World Politics*, edited by R. O. Keohane and J. S. Nye, Jr., ix-xxix. Cambridge: Harvard University Press.

O'Connor, J. 1970. "The Meaning of Economic Imperialism." In *Imperialism and*

Underdevelopment, edited by R. Rhodes, 101–50. New York: Monthly Review Press.

Papanek, G. F. 1973. "Aid, Foreign Private Investment, Savings, and Growth in Less Developed Countries." *Journal of Political Economy* 81: 120–30.

Pinelo, A. 1973. *The Multinational Corporation as a Force in Latin American Politics: A Case Study of the International Petroleum Company in Peru*. New York: Praeger.

Pinto, A. 1974. "Economic Relations Between Latin America and the United States." In *Latin America and the United States: The Changing Political Realities*, edited by J. Cotler and R.R. Fagen, 100–16. Stanford, Calif.: Stanford University Press.

Polachek, S. W. 1980. "Conflict and Trade." *Journal of Conflict Resolution* 24 (March): 55–78.

Portes, A. 1976. "On the Sociology of National Development: Theories and Issues." *American Journal of Sociology* 82: 55–85.

Przeworski, A., and H. Teune. 1970. *The Logic of Comparative Social Inquiry*. New York: Wiley.

Ranis, G. 1976. "The Multinational Corporation as an Instrument of Development." In *The Multinational Corporation and Social Change*, edited by D. E. Apter and L. W. Goodman, 96–117. New York: Praeger.

Ray, D. 1973. "The Dependency Model of Latin American Underdevelopment: Three Basic Fallacies." *Journal of InterAmerican Studies and World Affairs* 15: 4–20.

Reuber, G. L. 1973. *Private Foreign Investment in Development*. Oxford: Clarendon Press.

Richardson, N. R. 1976. "Political Compliance and U.S. Trade Dominance." *American Political Science Review* 70 (December): 1098–1109.

———. 1978. *Foreign Policy and Economic Dependence*. Austin: University of Texas Press.

Richardson, N. R., and C. W. Kegley, Jr. 1980. "Trade Dependence and Foreign Policy Compliance: A Longitudinal Analysis." *International Studies Quarterly* 24 (June): 191–222.

Rothgeb, J. M. Jr. 1982–83. "Contagion at the Sub-War Stage: Siding in the Cold War, 1959–1963." *Conflict Management and Peace Science* 6 (March): 39–58.

———. 1984a. "The Effects of Foreign Investment on Overall and Sectoral Growth in Third World States." *Journal of Peace Research* 21: 5–16.

———. 1984b. "Investment Penetration in Manufacturing and Extraction and External Public Debt in Third World States." *World Development* 12 (November/December): 1063–76.

———. 1984–85. "The Contribution of Foreign Investment to Growth in Third World States." *Studies in Comparative International Development* 12 (Winter): 3–37.

———. 1986a. "Compensation or Opportunity: The Effects of International Recessions upon Direct Foreign Investment and Growth in Third World States, 1970–1978." *International Studies Quarterly* 30 (June): 123–152.

———. 1986b. "Testing Alternative Conceptions of the Relationship Between Direct Foreign Investment and Debt in Poor Countries." *Comparative Political Studies* 19 (April): 130–76.

———. 1987. "Trojan Horse, Scapegoat, or non–Foreign Entity: Foreign Policy and Investment Penetration in Poor Countries." *Journal of Conflict Resolution* 31 (June): 227–65.

Rothstein, R. 1977. *The Weak in the World of the Strong*. New York: Columbia University Press.

Rubinson, R. 1976. "The World Economy and the Distribution of Income Within States: A Cross-National Study." *American Sociological Review* 41 (August): 638–69.

———. 1977. "Dependence, Government Revenue, and Economic Growth, 1955–1970." *Studies in Comparative International Development* 12 (Winter): 3–28.

Senghaas, D. 1975. "Multinational Corporations and the Third World. On the problem of the further integration of peripheries into the given structure of the international economic system." *Journal of Peace Research* 12 (no. 4): 257–74.

Sklar, R. L. 1975. *Corporate Power in an African State*. Berkeley, University of California Press.

Spanier, J. 1978. *Games Nations Play*. New York: Praeger.

Spencer, M. H. 1974. *Contemporary Economics*. New York: Worth.

SPSS, Inc. 1983. *SPSSX User's Guide*. New York: McGraw-Hill.

Staley, E. 1979. "Conditions under Which Investments Are Most Frequently Involved in Political Friction." In *Transnational Corporations and World Order*, edited by G. Modelski, 187–204. San Francisco: W. H. Freeman.

Sunkel, O. 1979. "Big Business and 'Dependencia.' " In *Transnational Corporations and World Order*, edited by G. Modelski, 216–25. San Francisco: W. H. Freeman.

Szymanski, A. 1976. "Dependence, Exploitation, and Economic Growth." *Journal of Political and Military Sociology* 4: 53–65.

Taylor, C., and M. Hudson. 1972. *World Handbook of Political and Social Indicators*. New Haven, Conn.: Yale University Press.

Vernon, R. 1971. *Sovereignty at Bay*. New York: Basic Books.

———. 1976. "Multinational Enterprises in Developing Countries: Issues in Dependency and Interdependence." In *The Multinational Corporation and Social Change*, edited by D. E. Apter and L. W. Goodman, New York: Praeger.

———. 1977. *Storm Over the Multinationals*. Cambridge, Mass.: Harvard University Press.

———. 1978–79. "Multinationals: No Strings Attached." In *Foreign Policy*, 33: 121–34.

———. 1981. "Sovereignty at Bay: Ten Years After." *International Organization* 35: 517–30.

Vincent, J. E. 1980. *Factor Analysis in International Relations*. Gainesville: University of Florida Press.

Waltz, K. 1970. "The Myth of National Interdependence." In *The International Corporation*, edited by C. P. Kindleberger, 205–23. Cambridge, Mass.: MIT Press.

Weinstein, F. B. 1976. "The Uses of Foreign Policy in Indonesia." *World Politics* 24: 356–81.

Weisskopf, T. E. 1972. "The Impact of Foreign Capital Inflow on Domestic Savings in Underdeveloped Countries." *Journal of International Economics* 2 (February): 25–38.

Wells, L. T., Jr. 1971. "The Multinational Business Enterprise: What Kind of International Organization?" In *Transnational Relations and World Politics*, edited by R. O. Keohane and J. S. Nye, Jr. 97–114. Cambridge, Mass.: Harvard University Press.

World Bank. 1976. *World Tables*. Baltimore: Johns Hopkins University Press.

———. 1980. *World Tables*. Baltimore: Johns Hopkins University Press.

———. 1983. *World Tables*. Baltimore: Johns Hopkins University Press.

Index

About the Author

JOHN M. ROTHGEB, JR., was born in Arlington, Virginia in 1949. He received his B.A. and M.A. in government from the College of William and Mary. His Ph.D. in political science is from the University of Kentucky. He currently is Associate Professor of Political Science at Miami University. He is the author of numerous articles on international development and conflict in leading political science, international relations, and international development journals.